Endorsements

I first met Robert just over two years ago now, when I answered the call to serve Northwest Christian Church of Arlington, Texas. Robert and his wife, Charlene, are members here, as well as other members of his extended family who have connections with the congregation. If I had to describe my relationship with Robert, it is one of evolving and progressive knowledge of the depth of his Christian journey.

You will read in this book of the incredibly varied life experiences with which Robert has journeyed—from birth to today. It is the depth and breadth of those experiences that make him the man, the Christian exemplar he is today.

As his pastor, I know Robert to be a deeply committed disciple of Christ Jesus, which informs his every experience and relationship. That knowledge assures me that the reading of his book will not only inform you about his journey but also inform and enrich your own.

May God's shalom be with you as you read and as you journey.

—Pastor David Hargrave

As I remember the old Sunday school song, "He Has the Whole World in His Hands," I think of our Savior's love for us, His embrace, His kindness to us, and above all—His amazing grace. If this book has taught us anything, let us embrace in our hearts and minds and our souls the very thoughts and experiences Robert Grant has lived out on his journey in life with all humbleness, meekness, and indulgence in faith and thanksgiving to our loving, caring, awesome God. What a fantastic testimony of faith, adventure, and adversity; a prime example of God's desire to be right there with His children from the beginning to the end. Thank you, Robert, for writing such a God-inspired, heartfelt autobiography!

—Rev. T. J. Lalonde

Touched by the Finger of God

The Heartfelt True Story of a Faithful Believer

ROBERT E. GRANT

WESTBOW
PRESS®
A DIVISION OF THOMAS NELSON
& ZONDERVAN

WestBow Press books may be ordered through booksellers or by contacting:

WestBow Press
A Division of Thomas Nelson & Zondervan
1663 Liberty Drive
Bloomington, IN 47403
www.westbowpress.com
1 (866) 928-1240

Scripture quotes are taken from the King James Version of the Bible.

ISBN: 978-1-5127-9465-6 (sc)
ISBN: 978-1-5127-9464-9 (e)

Library of Congress Control Number: 2017910403

Print information available on the last page.

WestBow Press rev. date: 7/7/2017

This book is especially dedicated to my lifelong companion, Charlene, of over forty-three years. As a special gift from God, she entered into my life in a unique way. I would not be able to survive without her wisdom and great personality. It is Charlene's numerous years of dedicated and relentless research that enabled the reuniting of my biological family. It is her love of family that has led to the creation of this book. Thank you, Charley, for supporting and loving me all of these years!

Contents

Acknowledgments

Without the diligent support and continued encouragement from so many friends and family members, I may not have drummed up the courage to sit down and write this book. I want to extend my sincere gratitude to all of those who have given me the courage and constant prompting to share the special life events that have made a difference in many lives and certainly mine. I pray this book will change at least one life for the better and will turn many who are undecided to follow Jesus Christ our Savior.

I wish to extend my sincerest gratitude to my eldest brother, Reverend T. J. Lalonde, for his commitment to this project and for sharing his extensive knowledge of the Bible. His continual years of studying and sharing the Bible have given many a closer walk with God. I have greatly benefited from his love of our Lord and the Bible, as we shared numerous special moments of reading and learning God's Word together.

In addition, I want to extend a special thanks to my daughter-in-law, Kim, who has a remarkable, natural artistic talent. Her dedication to illustrating one of the book's special meanings through her artwork is no doubt a blessing indeed!

We send our love and gratitude to Pastor David Hargrave who has blessed our family tremendously with his presence and counsel during some of our most enjoyable and sensitive moments. He is truly an exceptional and dedicated minister and a great friend in Christ.

The following life story is true; however, I have changed some of the names of those involved in the events to protect their identities. Sit back and enjoy. I pray there will be something within the book that may help to change your life for the better and bring you closer to our Lord.

Author's Special Message

I have written this faith-based book as my testimony of the many miracles that have occurred in my life. It is evident to me that miracles and other blessed events do exist in every one of our lives, and often on an ongoing basis. Whether they are extraordinary or just simply a minute part of a life event, God inspires them all. These special life moments are divinely designed and inserted within our lives in an effort to bring us closer to Him. All we are required to do is trust in our Lord, let Him perform His wonders, and pray to Him constantly. Just as He provides for the smallest animal or bird, He will always provide for us and will continue to show us His glory and power. He is an awesome God, and He loves each of us tremendously.

It is through God's love and through the power of the Holy Spirit within me that I share this testimony. As I have learned from my life experiences, it is important to take the time to ... be still and know that He is God. We must believe in the miracles God is revealing to us and inserts into our lives, no matter how they present themselves. It is important that we take these special events and learn from them. We need to share these experiences with our families and others so that they too will believe in God's almighty powers and presence. Our heavenly Father is very well alive and is lovingly at work within our daily lives.

For those separated from parents and/or siblings, I pray you will not give up the dream of someday reuniting with them. God works miracles, and if it is His will, you will be a reunited family again.

> For ye have not received the spirit of bondage again to fear; but ye have received the Spirit of adoption, whereby we cry, Abba, Father.
> —Romans 8:15 (KJV)

In the Beginning
Ω

It is a reoccurring black-and-white dream that has always astounded me. Is it just a back-of-the-mind dream with no merit? On the other hand, my conscience replays an actual event every time I go to sleep. Have you ever had a dream where you see yourself and those around you as clearly as though you are right there?

My dream begins in the backseat of an auto. From the look of the cars and the dress of the characters, the era must be the fifties. It is dark outside, and I can see the streetlights going by swiftly as I lie down in the backseat of a cold and noisy vehicle. I have no idea where I am or where I have been; nor do I know where I am going. I feel a little frightened, but then again, I am not too worried as long as I am in the dark and hidden from clear view. As the streetlights continue going by, each one lights up the interior of the vehicle just enough to cast shadows on the seats. I continue to doze in and out of sleep. I feel tired and cannot hold my eyes open. I must be only a few years old, as my thoughts are pure yet meaningless. The continual pitter-patter of the raindrops against the car window provides a mellow song as the darkness grows longer. Where am I? Who am I?

Eager to learn more, I want to catch a glimpse of the shapes of those in the front seat each time the lights shine within the car. It is a mystery to be resolved later, who these two people are as they drive for what seems to be an eternity. They are driving steadily into the night, not stopping and not sleeping.

As usual, I have awakened once again, only to discover the dream reoccurred without a conclusion and without answers to my questions. I have had this same dream for many years now. In the late 1990s, my adopted parents finally took the time to listen patiently as I repeated the dream to them. I was determined to get some sort of explanation as to what it meant. I prayed they could end my never-ending quest to find the answers to this mysterious saga.

After years of pondering the reality of my dream, I found it to be an actual past event. My final adoptive parents were the mysterious persons in the car. It had been raining as they drove for hours from out of state to Richland Hills, Texas. I became a new member of their family, and for the third and final time, I had a permanent home. This place turned out to be a real home where I began to grow up, learning about life, living within a stable family, and learning about God. It became a home where every day in my life was a learning process. In addition, this is where the mysterious miracles and blessed moments in my life began to occur.

I became an inhabitant of this somewhat humane society. Unplanned perhaps, but at least my biological mom had decided to accept and carry me to birth. Giving birth to a child is very challenging, and the decision to keep this precious life is not only the right choice but also a blessing to all. A baby is a special gift from God that no one should take for granted. Nonetheless, for better or worse, my appearance in this world was destined to happen. God knew what He was going to do with my life. I had no clue as to when or how these remarkable events in my life would soon start to take place. God's plans for me would be slowly revealed over the next forty-something years. What a revelation He gave! His actions have been nothing short of one miracle after another. I am very blessed and fortunate to have a God that loves me so much and gives of Himself continually.

After many years of research, we discovered my biological parents as Leroy, of Upstate New York, and Rosie, a strong-willed young woman of Bridgeport, Texas. Dad, who died in 1995, was a guitar player who spent a lot of time traveling the circuit, often referred to as the "circus." He would sometimes stray away from home and play with upcoming country and western gigs. He used the circuit as a means of getting across country to follow his dreams. Dad thought his best talent was yodeling and singing, but a recently discovered 45 rpm proves otherwise. He had the pleasure of playing with Tex Ritter on numerous occasions and charmingly stole Mom's heart.

Mom and Leroy wound up heading toward Sydney, New York. Eventually, they moved back to Bridgeport for a short while and then decided to move to Martinez, California. As time went by, they were somewhat blessed with several children. In 1953, I was born in Vallejo, California, at a small general hospital that had a fire several years later. My quick entrance into this world seemed a bit mysterious and sketchy due to the lack of supporting documentation. Unfortunately, I had become a potential "nobody" due to the lost records from the fire that destroyed the hospital. It is not for certain if any records were saved from the blaze. However, in later years, Charlene and I discovered some of the unknowns in my life within one of the secretive, big, blacked-out books held by the California adoption system.

Mom, on the other hand, came from a large family of eleven siblings who were dirt poor but rich in family roots. Her father was a hardworking man, but as an alcoholic, he brought many challenges to the family. The stress of living with an alcoholic is not fun and is hard on all family members. Her mother was strict but an innocent soul doing her best to help raise a large family on a small budget. Her hands were marked with the years of preparing meals, washing dishes, and mending clothes.

3

Mom met Leroy when he came passing through Bridgeport, Texas, looking for work. She was so ready to leave Bridgeport and wanted out of town no matter what. She had a hard time trying to cope with the many family issues that anything outside of town would be greener pastures. Several of the other siblings in the household had the same desire to move on. Some of them left school at an early age to find happiness and a better future. Some of the siblings joined the service, while others left for distant opportunities, only to return to Bridgeport or the surrounding area later in life. One of the siblings, George, moved to Guam to raise a family and never returned to Texas.

Life in California did not go as anticipated; Dad could not find steady work, causing him to not always stay on the right track in life. He had once "borrowed" a license plate for his own vehicle and found himself in trouble with the law. He always seemed to find trouble and developed a taste for alcohol. It is my understanding he had an affair. This is when Mom decided it was time for her and the four children to return to Bridgeport. This once-upon-a-time love affair between Dad and Mom sadly ended soon after I was born. Hearts were broken. The distant relationship increasingly dismantled itself, and the two finally separated forever.

As a result, Dad moved back to Upstate New York and finally settled down after marrying a wonderful woman who did her best to keep him in line. Another set of children made its way into this hard and cruel world. This once beloved Texas connection would now be forgotten for several years to come.

In her defense, Mom had it tough trying to make ends meet, earning as much as two dollars a night in tips as a server in a bar and grill in Fort Worth. Frantically, she would find places for all four of us kids to stay while she worked. Whenever possible, she would work overtime just to get enough money for food and to keep the bills paid. Sometimes it would be several days before she would make it back to pick us up and take us home. Times were hard, but she never gave up. Being a single mother is a full-time job with little respect and very little time for oneself. While living in an unforgiving society, it was hard to keep afloat in such situations.

Then one day a local family court made the decision to break up our family bonding. Our sibling hearts were broken in two, and Mom was heart sickened. My older siblings, Darlene and Darwin, were adopted by a family living in Dallas County. Our youngest sister headed in another direction to Hurst, Texas. Still just a toddler, I went several different directions before I was given to the Lena Pope home in Fort Worth. After a lengthy search, I was assigned to a foster family. I must have gone several different directions before my adoption by a wonderful young couple, the Grants, from Richland Hills, Texas. The court never released to the public the reasoning used to make its verdict. I am sure there were underlying factors that warranted the split. The hearing took place in Tarrant County, Texas. The adoption records were sealed, making the court's reasoning restricted from public access. Both Mom and our youngest sister's adoptive parents, the Wilsons, tried to regain custody of me, but the court would not allow it. In 1956, the Grants found an article in a Fort Worth newspaper. The story reflected on the events that had led to the permanent adoptions.

Can a woman forget her sucking child, that she
should not have compassion on the son of her womb?
Yea, they may forget, yet will I not forget thee.
—Isaiah 49:15 (KJV)

Robert Age 2

A Place to Call Home
Ω

Dad Grant was an upcoming and talented grocery man from day one. He was finally making his executive debut with a large grocery firm, Buddies Supermarkets, and was becoming very successful. He was a good-looking young man from Maypearl, Texas, who fell in love with his beautiful high school sweetheart. They had just moved into their new home in Richland Hills when they discovered adoption was the only way they could possibly have children.

One busy day, Dad Grant asked a collections officer to track down a hot check writer that owed the firm one hundred dollars (the equivalent of a thousand-dollar check today.) A few weeks later, my foster parents, who had written the bad check, were systematically located out of state. Like many poor families of the time, they were having financial problems. As a temporary solution toward making ends meet, they earned money by fostering children. However, they were in big trouble with the state of Texas for taking fostered children out of the state without permission. At this time, I was a ward of the state and was technically considered kidnapped.

Soon the check collector reported his findings to Dad Grant, who immediately contacted an attorney to go forth with an adoption. Thus, my unusual travels over the years led me to Richland Hills and a permanent home ... a real home. Finally I had an identity with

7

a solid name and a decent family! Suddenly, being three years old was not so bad after all. And at least I was worth a hundred dollars!

Now one of the questions resulting from the reoccurring dream would be answered. The Grants were the ones who were traveling the long distance out of state to pick me up and take me back to Texas. A judge gave them permission to foster me until a legal adoption was arranged through the Tarrant County court system. The adoption would eventually take place a couple of years later. Several divinely guided events had to occur before the big day in court.

I soon learned that being a kid in a big house with a huge yard and plenty of places to run and hide was not so bad. (As a little boy, the house seemed like a mansion, but after revisiting this boyhood home, I found the abode to be a small home for a family of five. The house is obviously less than 1,000 square feet, and the yard is a normal-sized neighborhood lot.) It occurred to me at the time that it was not important who I was or where I had traveled in the past. This did not matter, as I had a permanent home now, with new clothes and a red toy tractor! What more could a towheaded little boy desire?

It was not long before another little Irish boy from Dublin, Ireland, joined the family. Noel Anthony came to live with us from a Catholic orphanage. He was about three years younger than I was. Later in life, I discovered that Mom and Dad Grant had been trying to adopt Noel for a couple of years, but the orphanage was having difficulties getting Noel to the United States. Dad Grant had made several uneventful flights to New York, expecting each trip that Noel would be waiting for him. The Grants had given up on the adoption, which is why I was going to be officially adopted. (Since Noel had not shown up, all hope was lost, so the Grants decided to seek out another child.) Then, in 1957, just before my adoption hearing was to be held, the Grants got a call that Noel finally made it to New York, as a two-year-old, and they could not turn him down. Therefore, they adopted both of us during the same hearing in Fort Worth, Texas.

Noel became not just a brother but also a good friend. I always feared he would not stay for a long time and would be moving on, just as I had done previously. Soon after his arrival, the Grant family attended the adoption proceedings at a Tarrant County family court. I remember how dark, musty, and cold it was that day. There were several people in the darkened room. The judge let Noel and I sit on top of his bench! How cool was that? I remember looking at the audience and seeing many strange people in the courtroom. (As fate has it, this was not going to be my last appearance in a dark courtroom. This will become relevant later in the book.)

It seemed as though we were in the courtroom forever, but when the serious matters were completed, Noel and I were officially brothers. Finally, the Grants had legally adopted us both! Somehow, I had this feeling the Grants knew a few of the people in the courtroom. I can remember while we were still toddlers, Mom Grant in her excitement of having two boys always took pride in dressing us like twins. It was cute, but it became old for us boys after a while.

> And whoso shall receive one such little child in my name receiveth me.
> —Matthew 18:5 (KJV)

Life as a Grant
Ω

It was not long before Noel and I were attending public school in Richland Hills. We had our beginnings with the Birdville Independent School System. Our childhood "mansion" was a mile or so from the local Glenview Elementary. Going there made us feel so grown-up. The school building had several rooms but no air-conditioning. It is a good thing the building had many windows, as floor fans were hard to come by in those days. At the time we started public school, Mom Grant also had us attending Catholic education classes at our church school (St. John's) across the street from Glenview. It seemed like forever and a day before I graduated from both schools. Noel and I felt as though we were getting overeducated! In addition, the nuns at St. John's were very strict on discipline … no horse playing was allowed around there! Despite the extra class hours, our additional education was meaningful to us. How quickly we realized the importance of religious education within the family.

A kid didn't get much rest around the Grant family, as there was always work like pulling weeds, mowing yards, sweeping, doing dishes, dusting, doing laundry, cleaning bathrooms, and whatever else needed to be done. The two of us boys had to do it before we could play or go to bed. Did I mention homework? That too, and lots of it! Saturdays could not come soon enough! Once the chores were completed, it was out the back door and off to Never Never Land! We must have been a dirty family, as Mom Grant did not let up on the constant cleaning. We only had one tub, so keeping it clean was a major priority. She even taught us how to wash and iron our own clothes!

Nonetheless, Noel and I always had a great time as we wandered all over Richland Hills. Just as long as we returned home for supper, we were free to roam and explore. Mom Grant would make us sack lunches to take along on our excursions. This was smart, as all of that hiking just made us starve! In today's world, it would almost be forbidden to go off wandering for hours to soak up adventures just like Huckleberry Finn.

We always met new friends in the neighborhood since we spent most of our time outdoors. At one time, there were more than eighteen kids in the neighborhood! On a usual day, we would all get together and do things like have a boxcar derby. Even our sweet little girly next-door neighbor would participate! There were more boys in the neighborhood, so we would let her tag along, and usually she became better than most of us guys at everything we did! The street we lived on had a small decline at the end of the road. Everyone would take turns riding our home-made racing cars down the road and then toting them back up the hill just to ride them downhill all over again. We spent hours having fun even though cuts and bruises were inevitable. A few knocked-out teeth and broken bones were symbols of our heroic actions!

Noel and I had a cool racing car made with old lawnmower wheels that Granddad Johnson (Mom Grant's father) gave us. We used old wood two-by-fours for axles that we would maneuver by using our feet to turn left or right. We tried making stick brakes, but they never worked. Therefore, the boy thing to do was to crash into a tree or just use our feet to stop. We tore up a lot of skin doing that, as we never wore our good school shoes. Mom Grant would have had us shot dead if we were caught wearing our good school shoes outside to play!

Growing up with Noel was so much fun, as we spent a lot of time hiking during the summer and climbing just about every tree in town. We always chose the taller and more dangerous trees. They were far more fun to climb, and the higher we could get, the better! One day, Noel and I took a map of the city and walked the entire perimeter! We walked along railroad tracks, along creek beds, and down the busy highways. What a hike! Nevertheless, we always made it back home in time for supper.

During the summer, our favorite nighttime thing to do was to sleep outside in our hammocks that Dad Grant strung between the large, fruitless mulberry trees in our backyard. Many nights we would stay awake just to watch the stars fall, the planes fly over, and the UFOs dancing across the skies. Never once were we afraid of anything. Being boys meant growing up to become strong-willed men without fear of evil men, aliens, or monsters crawling over the yard fence at night!

In 1964, when I was around eight years old, Mom and Dad Grant were blessed with their first biological son, Sidney Paul. I was now a big brother to two younger brothers. What a wonderful feeling having a growing family. Until Sid was old enough to run with Noel and me, we spent a lot of time with our grandparents in order to give Mom Grant some down time.

We focused all of our attention on the little fellow. It was so awesome to have Sid in our lives, as he completed our unique family of five. Nothing like having the familiar *My Three Sons* in our household. He was continuously ill from day one, most likely because of his premature size. His constant care was necessary to help him gain strength and weight. It took all of us to love Sid and to take care of him. Nothing like having a baby brother!

Noel and I did not know what to think about this little man. He was a very premature baby, and neither one us thought he would ever grow up. As older brothers, we felt it was our job to take care of little Sid. The older he became, the more we loved him. Naturally, he always wanted to hang around with his two bigger brothers because he felt safe. (Well semi-safe anyway.) We were so wild; little Sid was always getting hurt. If he was not getting an arm broken from being pushed out of the tree house, then he was getting hurt while playing baseball, or he was getting his teeth knocked out. Yep, it was our duty as bigger brothers to take "good care" of him!

It is a wonder Sid survived at all. I can remember pulling him in our red Ryder wagon one day, going a little too fast in order to excite him, but knocking out his teeth when the wagon abruptly turned over. Man, did I ever feel bad about that! I hurt even more when Mom and Dad Grant got around to almost killing me. From then on, we were more careful not to hurt the poor kid.

Sid, as a young child, was diagnosed with St. Vitus Dance, a curable disease where nonvoluntary jolting of the arms and legs occur. We were so glad he would get the right treatments, leading to a quick recovery. We all felt so badly for him because we knew the medication was not pleasant. He could not play with us as usual until his illness was showing signs of improvement, which seemed like forever. We really missed him hanging around with us.

Soon after the "dance," we discovered he had a cyst on the backside of one of his knee joints, thus requiring surgery. Eventually Sid grew up to overcome his many childhood illnesses. Today, Sid is a very good-looking young man and is strong as an ox. It must have been all of those protein drinks he was required to drink while younger in order to gain muscle and weight.

Noel and I spent our best summers at our Granddad and Grandma Johnson's house in River Oaks. They had a close neighbor boy nicknamed Tater. He was an angler to the bone! Tater could fish with anything and catch just about any kind of fish swimming around in the West Fork of the Trinity River. Prior to going fishing on one of our daily excursions, we would take cornflakes, mix them with water in a jar, and let them sit overnight in order to make the best bait for catfish. We would then take the cornflake mush, shape it into a ball, and place it on our hooks. The catfish were in heaven, as the bait would simply fall off after a few minutes of soaking in the river. Sometimes, if the bait held long enough, we would get lucky and catch a big one!

Occasionally, the river would be fierce with currents, especially after it rained. It was then Grandma would tell us not to go into the water, but nothing would stop us from a day of seining for minnows to go fishing. Grandma could smell catfish on us a mile away, so we would always stay down at the river long enough to dry out. Somehow, she always knew what we had done, so we would spend the next day on the front porch of the house—grounded. I guess the West Fork of the Trinity must have stunk pretty badly!

Nevertheless, after a day's worth of being porch grounded, Grandma would let us go fishing again. I figured we were enough trouble to her sitting around the house, so it was a blessing to get us out of her hair for a day. Boys will be boys. Swimming in the river to cool off was always tempting and rewarding after a hard day of grounding.

One day, however, the river life did not seem so inviting. We had heard a huge carp had eaten a man. It was so large it had pulled him into the river while he was fishing. We spent days watching the river to see if this monster would show up. Then finally the water in the river had drained so low we could see an object washed up on a sandbar downstream. We went closer to get a better look, and sure enough, it was the carp with its head cut off. This river monster was about four feet long but certainly not big enough to eat a man. Unless it had chewed him up really, really well!

All the kids in my grandparents' neighborhood were good

friends. We spent our late evenings playing baseball in one of the local backyards. Even the girls got into the action. We were all so poor; very few of us had ball gloves, so the softball was our choice for the games. The only bad thing about playing the game in the backyards was the stickers. It seemed like every yard had those horrible, annoying things. Most of us kids did not wear shoes, so getting stickers in the feet made the games hazardous and a brutal challenge. I have had my fill of those annoying things. Eventually my feet were calloused enough to withstand the pain a little better than most of the other players.

However, I was not as tough skinned as I had believed. I can remember one day Grandma Johnson telling me not to go play in the next-door neighbor's yard, as they really had a mess of fresh stickers. Nevertheless, being a hardheaded sandpit kid, I was determined to play ball. It quickly became the most humiliating day of my life. After finding my way to the outfield, it occurred to me I had to go to the restroom. The feeling was so strong that I ran toward Grandma's house and right into a big, relentless patch of those barbaric things! They hurt so bad I lost control and wet all over myself, with girls and boys laughing during every minute of my agonizing pain. I never wanted to play ball again, especially when the girls were around. It seemed to take hours for Grandad Johnson to help me yank all of those annoying things out of my feet. My feet ached for days after, and walking was so painful. Word of advice ... never underestimate the wisdom of a grandmother and always take heed of what she tells you.

> She opens her mouth with wisdom, and the
> teaching of kindness is on her tongue.
> —Proverbs 31:26 (KJV)

A Flower Garden
Ω

When I was young boy around the age of nine or ten, I wanted a flower garden to call my very own. After pleading with Mom Grant, she finally gave in and allowed me to take a small area in our backyard to plant my first flower garden. I guess my persistent nagging finally wore her down to the point of saying, "All right, go ahead."

On a bright sunny day, she helped me to plant some zinnias. I could not wait to see the multiple colors and to show off my hard work. Mom Grant had lectured me as to how I should keep the weeds pulled, thus cautioning me to be careful to not pull out the baby flower growths.

Then one day, a friend who lived across the street from us came over to play. I told him about my newly planted flower garden and how Mom Grant showed me what to do to keep the weeds out and when to water. The fellow proceeded to confuse me by saying I had nothing but weeds in the garden, and he pulled out about half of the growths before I could get Mom Grant to come out and check on him.

Boy was I in trouble! You would have thought I had killed a million trees! She sent the boy home and sent me to my room. This once-considered good friend had misguided and tricked me. After this misguided ordeal, I would not let the kid back in our yard for months! He betrayed me one too many times, and I usually wound up in serious trouble. I may have been ignorant, but I was not going to let him take advantage of me ever again.

Mom Grant sent me to my room while baby Sid and Noel went to visit with her as she folded clothes. They were having a great time talking and cutting up while I cried my heart out all alone in my darkened room. How could God be so cruel to let me get into so much trouble? How could He let a little boy lose his first garden, especially after begging for days to get it? The longer I stayed sitting in my lonely room against the bedroom wall, the longer I sulked, the more I cried, and the madder I became at God.

I was a good Christian boy and did everything I could to behave, to do right, to go to church on Sundays, to attend Christian classes, and to make great grades at school. (In today's world, I might be considered a Goody Two-shoes or a nerd.) Now what more did God (or any parent) want from a kid like me? How could He let such a terrible thing like this happen? Why was I the one to get into trouble and not the kid across the street? Just like any typical kid, I was furious and did not think my punishment was fair.

Then it happened. Slowly, my little-boy striped T-shirt lifted upward on my back by itself, as I somewhat gently leaned against the wall. I had never felt so scared in my life. A soft but definite sign of the cross was gently impressed upon my back. I took a moment for complete silence. No more tears and no more anger. In a solemnly quiet moment, a startling moment of disbelief came over me as a thousand thoughts raced in my mind. *Should I turn around? Should I run away? Should I touch the wall? Should I pray for forgiveness as God may doom me forever?* My mind raced as deep fear began to set in. Had I committed the ultimate sin? Did I dare talk to God in such a manner? On the other hand, was it really God?

I quietly said, "God, if that was you and not the devil, would you do that again?" I quietly waited for a response. What would happen next? I was shaking and felt very cold as I leaned against the wall with the fear of moving. My body could not move, as though someone or something had glued it to the floor. Would I be pulled into the wall and disappear forever? Was I to die for sinning against God? Deep inside, I was stricken with fear, but in a strange way, I had a sense of peace.

And again, as gentle as once before, the precious finger of God pressed His mark upon my boney little back, as if to say, "I understand. I am sorry for your suffering, and I will love you always."

At that moment, I felt relieved and yet deeply sorry for what I had just done. I cried even harder, asking God to forgive me and to be with me forever. I just wanted God to help this little boy to become whatever He wanted him to be. I wanted God to be with me too as I walked down the hallway to the room where Mom Grant and my brothers played. Would I still be in trouble? Would Mom Grant laugh at me? Would the others reject me? Would I be in more trouble than before? Would I be embarrassed and turned away in shame? Would I still receive a severe punishment when Dad Grant arrived home from work?

I did not want them to think I was crazy or just making up a story in order to seek acceptance from Mom Grant and to get out of my room with some kind of dignity. I wanted so badly for Mom Grant to see the suffering, but mostly the fear, I had just endured and yet to believe in me for once in my life—something my parents seldom showed toward this scrawny four-eyed kid.

As I sat and told my story, Mom Grant became convinced it was for real. If anything, the experience had touched and softened her heart as well. She knew too that this event had to be God reaching out to us all. Mom Grant believed me and felt the look of a scared little boy who had just experienced a miraculous moment with God. Little did she know how this special event would affect my life for years to come! From that day forward, Mom Grant actually took a different look toward me, and we became a lot closer than before. We began to build a trusting relationship and could talk about anything together with a mutual understanding and with love.

As I grew to become a teenager, one of our conversations involved Mom Grant telling me what she knew about my biological family. We had agreed not to let it become a big issue. Willingly, she offered to help me if I ever wanted to find my biological family. She definitely understood the importance of a child reconnecting to his or her biological family. As she put it, a child needs that special connection to his or her siblings and parents. As a teen, finding my biological family did not seem important, because I had the Grants as my immediate family. That was what really mattered to me most. Mom Grant, however, had given me a piece of paper listing what we thought was my biological sister's name and where we thought she lived. It was our belief that my sister may have been a twin. Uninterested at the time, I simply placed the paper in my wallet, realizing it was almost impossible to find my biological family.

Have you ever seen the plant known as the rose of Sharon? The Hebrew word for "Sharon" means a plain or a level place. The Plain of Sharon is a coastal plain between the mountains of central Palestine and the Mediterranean Sea, just north of Joppa to Mt. Carmel. It is mentioned in Acts 9:35 and in Isaiah 35:1.

The Song of Solomon 2:1 mentions the "Rose of Sharon" again, also known as Hibiscus syriacus. It is a beautiful green bush that yields a white, red, pink, and purple flower that grows very tall and thick. It is a source of saffron. Symbolically, as in reference to our Lord, the white stands for His purity; the red for His blood that was shed for our sins on the cross; the pink for His love and graciousness toward us; and finally the purple for his divine majesty and sovereignty as our Eternal King.

We are all part of God's great earthly garden—a vast array

of beautiful fragrant flowers ever reaching for the Son. Thus, the flower is adorned elegantly as the beautiful bride of the Father's precious Son, the rose of Sharon.

Here we have read about the innocence of a young boy, a child of God, exercising great faith and wisdom in crying out to the Father and requesting to know the very person who was touching him at that very moment. The Father recognized already this young man was displaying careful discernment in trying the spirits to see which was of God. This boy, although possessing a broken spirit and a saddened heart, was determined to get down to the matter at hand and to understand it truly was the Lord who had touched him. Therefore, with such tenderness, God touched him again. It was a powerful and spirit-filled moment between God and the boy who loves him so much. (In 1 John 4:1, the Bible cautions us to test the spirits, as there are many bad spirits that have been sent throughout the world, so we must be careful. Consider reading in the Bible about the young man of God, Samuel, in 1 Samuel 3.)

From that day of the sacred touching, my faith took a huge step forward as I began to realize how important it is to be aware of God. Our Lord does exist, and He hears and sees all things in our lives. As faithfully taught, during my earlier days of religious education, we are to fear the Lord. However, as an older adult, I have learned it is more important to have great faith in Him rather than to live in fear. God does not want to harm any of us because we are His children. If we show Him our love and live our lives devoted to Him, He will be the greatest Father, hands down.

> Call unto me, and I will answer thee, and show thee great and mighty things, which thou knowest not.
> —Jeremiah 33:3 (KJV)

A Divine Visit
Ω

It was not long after the flower garden incident that the remaining zinnias began to grow and became my pride and joy. The family watched the various colors become majestic and was amazed by how high they had grown. The plants continued to grow throughout the summer and into late fall. I knew why; call it divine intervention. I was so thankful the boy across the street did not totally ruin my garden. In addition, God came through on His promise to answer my prayers to let the garden survive. Even today, I plant zinnias around my mailbox as a reminder of that miraculous summer. Zinnias are one of God's replicas of the rainbow here on earth. We get to see the wonderful colors of the rainbow in the sky growing here on the ground. This is another reminder of His true love and covenant for us all. What an amazing gift to humanity.

Mom Grant had a little more faith in me from then on. I managed to get her to allow me to mow yards for our neighbors and to clean out their flowerbeds. I was able to start saving a few dollars to go see a movie or to get an occasional hamburger and shake at the local fountain store. Noel and I loved to ride our bikes to the Motts 5 and 10 on special days even though it was a long ride; it was worth every penny. They had the best shakes, and we could ponder over the plastic car, boat, and airplane models. They had hundreds! We could even get a great car model and glue for around a dollar.

Mom Grant was also good about telling us Bible stories, and we were all so intrigued with them. We loved to go indoors during the hot summer and listen to her talk about God. Imagine kids wanting to come inside to listen to religion on a summer day other than a Sunday!

One summer day, Mom Grant was talking to us kids when the doorbell chimed. Naturally, we all went to the door to see who was standing on the front porch. Usually, it was either a Fuller brush sales representative making his rounds or a "Charlie's" potato chip man, or even a milkman, all who would stop occasionally at our door to sell us goods.

However, not one of these solicited on this hot day. Mom opened the door, and we saw a man standing there wearing a heavy, black, hooded coat. His face did not show as he asked for some bread and water. (It was very strange to see someone wearing a long and heavy black coat this time of year.) Mom had not been to the store recently, and we only had a few slices of bread in the pantry. She told him to wait and she would be back with food.

She went into the kitchen to make him a sandwich and filled a cup with some juice or water. We all returned to the door as Mom gave him the food and drink. I remember to this day his face literally lit up with a glow as he thanked her and turned to go away. Naturally, being inquisitive kids, we ran out the back door, going different directions toward the front yard to get a glimpse of the man.

To our disappointment and surprise, he simply disappeared! No car, no bike. He was not walking, nor was he hiding. It was as though he had vanished. We all went back inside the house to tell Mom, and she looked as if she had seen a ghost! She told us boys about the biblical story of God knocking at the door. She warned us that day never to turn down anyone who is seeking food, as it could be one of God's angels! My heart was pounding so hard I could hear it. I will never forget the image of this possible angel standing on our front door step. Was God checking up on the family? Perhaps. Was God visiting us for a reason? Particularly, was God letting me know that He was still with me? I stayed awake for nights on end pondering the man at the door. Today my wife and I have a paper hand fan that has a picture of God knocking at the door hanging next to our front door entrance. It is a reminder of this mysterious day when Mom Grant taught us boys about this wonderful biblical story. We will always remember to be charitable and give to anyone knocking at our door. (Later in my life, this story of the knocking at the door came back to me at a time of pure joy, as I will share with you later in the book.)

> Let brotherly love continue. Be not forgetful to entertain strangers; for thereby some have entertained Angels unaware.
> —Hebrews 13:2 (KJV)

During another blazing summer vacation, I had the chance to spend a week after one of my birthdays with my grandparents. I was so happy because my parents let me take my brand-new bicycle. I loved it—a black and white Huffy bike with playing cards attached to strike the spokes as the wheels turned. I was uptown for a small boy. I am guessing I was around ten at the time. This bike was my first without training wheels, and it made me feel so special and grown-up.

After a hard day of playing at my grandparents' house, I was very tired and left my new bike on the driveway, leaning against their garage door. Their house was very tiny and sat on top of a hill in the south part of River Oaks near the West Fork of the Trinity River. The bike was next to the front porch so I could come out the front door early in the morning and jump right on it with little effort. My grandparents lived in a very old part of town, and the neighborhood was very down to earth and friendly. Few folks ever drove down this street. Thus, South River Oaks Blvd was the best-kept secret in all of town.

Grandmother Johnson had cautioned me not to leave the bike on the front porch several days before, and one night I simply failed to take it to the back porch. Yeah, I was a kid and did not think about the consequences of my actions. Then the inevitable happened.

Early the next morning, I went to get on my bike, but it was gone. I could not believe someone would take my bike! No one would expect this sort of action from this laid-back and loving neighborhood. It was a great, safe neighborhood. Everyone was honest. No one stole anything ... ever! No matter what, I believed this wholeheartedly.

I checked with our friend Tater from next door and the different neighbors to see if they saw anyone take my bike. Just perhaps someone may have borrowed it for a while. No one saw anything or borrowed the bike. The moment of realization and fear finally struck me, as I had to tell Grandma the bad news. She reminded me of what she told me just a few days before about taking the bike to the back porch each day.

Not only did I feel awful due to the loss of my bike, but I also feared what my parents were going to do to me once I returned home. Oh how I did not want to go home without that bike! My parents would definitely ground me for months, and I would never again get such a nice gift ... never!

I cried and cried my heart out and asked Grandmother to report it stolen as I also pleaded with her to help me find the bike. We both checked around the neighborhood again and gave the neighbors a description of the bike. We were determined to find out if anyone had seen any strange cars in the neighborhood or strange kids roaming the street.

Grandmother had always been a true Christian in every respect, and she believed in miracles. Her strong faith in God taught me how to pray. She urged me to pray with sincerity and from the heart. We prayed together the whole day. Praying with Grandmother was such a special moment, and I just knew God had to be listening to us both. I went to sleep that night asking God to help me find the bike, to forgive me for my sins, and to forgive me for not minding my grandparents. Once again, I went to sleep crying my eyes out, fearing the worst was yet to come.

The next morning came. I jumped out of bed and ran out the front door looking for the bike. It was not anywhere. Devastated, I once again came back inside the house feeling sick to my stomach, just knowing the bike was gone forever. How was I going to explain this to my parents? *God, didn't you hear our prayers? Did I pray in the wrong way or was I not sincere enough?*

I sat at the small kitchen table just barely eating my breakfast with Grandma, as Granddad had already left for work. We talked about normal everyday things, and I asked Grandmother if she would talk to my parents. I did not want them to kill me or ground me forever. I knew this was the last bike I would ever get. My life was going to be miserable from then on! We continued eating our breakfast and conversing about the recent tragedy.

Then suddenly we heard a knock at the front door. We went to see who might be there, and to our surprise, there was no one. We figured it must have been our imagination and continued into the kitchen to finish eating our breakfast. As soon as we sat down at the table, there was another knock at the door. We got up to answer it again, and one more time, no one was at the door. We looked outside to see if someone was standing in the yard or around the corner, and there was no one out there. We wondered if some kids were playing a dirty joke on us, but this would be very unusual.

I began to think about our safety and asked God to protect us. I had the weirdest feeling something was up but could not sense what. Once again, another knock at the door. Once again, we quickly opened the door just to find no one. However, this time God had answered my prayers! My bike! Amazingly, it returned to the exact same place and in the exact same position where I had left it a couple of days before!

We pondered over that situation and asked ourselves if someone could have been playing a trick on us. (Did my grandparents know where the bike was, or did they have a neighbor take it?) I will never know for sure, but in my heart that day, Grandmother and I both knew an angel had brought it back to us. I felt so much closer to Grandmother for enduring this dilemma with me. She appeared to be just as amazed about the returned bike. I did not let that bike out of my sight after that. It only takes one event like this to make a believer out of me. Just surviving the after-the-fact parental lecture later received was enough punishment to last a lifetime. Whew! What a lesson indeed! Truly, our God works in strange ways, and He certainly knows how to take care of undeserving kids! I never left the bike around front again and always put it inside the garage when I was not riding. This boy had learned a valuable lesson and became a sincere believer in praying!

Prayer works! This bike event is just another example of angels working on our behalf. For an interesting reading on angels who work on our behalf, go to the article "Angels to the Rescue" at heavenshelpers. org, as these spirit-filled stories will enlighten you further.

Tearfully I prayed, "Thank you, our Lord, for always being beside us to protect and to give us hope and peace within our hearts. In addition, Father, for giving us angels to help look out for us. Amen!"

> And whatsoever ye shall ask in my name, that will
> I do, that the Father may be glorified in the Son. If
> ye shall ask any thing in my name, I will do it.
> —John 14:13–14 (KJV)

Learning about Death
Ω

Time continued to move forward, and growing up seemed to be getting harder each day, especially when it came to losing friends and family. In 1986, when I was in the ninth grade, I had the privilege to become friends with a boy who lived about a mile from our home. I cannot remember his real name, so I will call him James. James had very few friends, mostly because he was severely handicapped. He was born with a rare form of bone cancer that was mind-boggling to the medical profession at the time. He was bound to a wheelchair and a neck brace. Due to these limiting restrictions, other kids had little to do with him.

I met James at school one day and instantly had a great friend. I went to his home several times during our brief friendship. His folks were the best, and they treated me with genuine love and courtesy. They were awesome folks.

I had never met anyone as genius as James. He could answer just about any question that would pop into my head. Questions like, how does a radio work? Or what is a planet made of? He could solve hard math questions from college texts. He showed me how to research all kinds of subject matter before the computer age and simply breathed intelligence. It was always great to spend time with James, as he taught me so much. Taking the mile-long bicycle ride to his home was well worth the effort because I knew James would be glad to see me. He always treated me like a best friend.

The saddest day in my boyhood life was when Mom Grant told me James had suddenly died. My heart broke into a million pieces that day. His loss filled me with so much anger. If only there was something I could have done to help save him. Did I do my best to be a good friend to him? Even though I had not known James very long, he had become the best friend anyone could have wanted.

James's parents wanted me to be a pallbearer at his funeral. I had never done anything of the sort in my life and was literally scared to death to be one. Mom Grant explained to me what I had to do and dressed me in my Sunday suit for the funeral. I remember being the youngest pallbearer of the group. Honorably, James was buried in the Bluebonnet Hills Cemetery near Colleyville, Texas.

That was the longest and hardest funeral to attend, as I can remember. It was so hard for James's parents to endure, and I could not imagine the heartbreak of burying a child. To this day, I do not like funerals, as they are so sad. Nonetheless, I think God was preparing me for what would take place later in my life.

The Bible tells us, "It is appointed unto men once to die, but after this the judgment" (Hebrews 9:27, KJV). The Bible helps us to accept the tragedy of death by teaching us what we would never expect to hear—that death is good, and for the most, it is a precious gift from God.

Romans 6:23 tells us, "The wages of sin is death; but the gift of God is Eternal Life through Jesus Christ our Lord" (KJV). Death has been the consequence of sin since the fall in the Garden of Eden. Death brings us separation and sorrow. Even our Lord Jesus (liken unto us) did not look forward to death, saying, "Oh my Father, if it be possible, let this cup pass from me" (Matthew 26:39, KJV). He was, however, quite confident in knowing He would be raised from the dead. Moreover, for those who believe in Him, they receive eternal life, a precious, gracious gift from God the Father.

I doubt very seriously that James sinned in his life simply because of his condition and restricted lifestyle. However, I do believe that by his dying, God gave James a new unrestricted eternal life in heaven, free from pain and suffering. I bet James is picking the brains of everyone in heaven, trying to absorb as much knowledge as possible. Someday, my good friend, we shall meet each other again.

> And God shall wipe away all the tears from their eyes; and there shall be no more death, neither sorrow, nor crying, neither shall there be any more pain: for the former things are passed away.
> —Revelation 20:4 (KJV)

Troubling Times
Ω

As we were growing up, Noel began to have serious mental problems. He was getting into trouble at school and disobeying everyone. Mom and Dad Grant would stay up late at night talking with him. They were trying to get him to understand he had to follow rules and stay out of trouble. It was not long afterward that Noel began to startle me in the mornings by pounding my chest for no apparent reason. We shared a bedroom, and eventually I became very afraid of him. Sometimes I would stay awake at night and wonder if or when he was going to attack me. I was slowly losing my childhood friend. God, what was wrong with Noel? What was happening to him?

I started to feel left out of the attention arena with our parents as time passed. Perhaps this is a prominent feeling among adopted siblings. There seemed to be less one-on-one time for me, and I started to feel as though I was becoming sort of an outsider. With issues surrounding Noel at hand, my adoptive parents had to spend a lot of their time focusing on resolving his problems. I felt so bad for him.

These troubling times ignited thoughts of my dismal childhood. The only remembrance of my toddler years was when I was accidently knocked across a room by my biological dad and received a nasty cut after hitting a bedpost. Similar memories led me to become somewhat of a recluse. Out of fear of being punished or literally kicked out of the home, I started to keep a very low profile. It became such a major fear; I became very careful of my actions and words, almost becoming silent and invisible. I tried to block out the memories that I hated the most and keep a positive outlook on life. I became shy at school and had few friends that I trusted to accept me and not harm me.

Mom and Dad Grant sent Noel to several doctors to help determine what was going wrong with him. With little advancement in his diagnosis, they eventually turned to a psychologist for help. Noel was given tranquilizers to control his mood swings and temper. However, these were just a temporary fix and caused him to be in a state of zombielike moods and behavior. Not a good way to go forward.

Sometimes Noel would feel great and somewhat normal. He would play and have a great time being himself. At other times, he was too sleepy or weary to function. We all became worried about his well-being and as to how long to continue this path of treatment. Noel did not seem to be happy, and his terrible fits of anger and physical abuse became more frequent and more violent.

Because of this uncontrollable behavior, it was not long before Mom and Dad Grant decided to send him to a Catholic boarding school in the Ozark Mountains near Searcy, Arkansas. He lived there for three years until he was too old to attend the school. Occasionally Dad and I would fly in a small corporate jet to go see him. He always seemed to be excited to see us and to tell us everything he was learning about the wilderness. However, he was different. Noticeably different. Perhaps I was being a little too perceptive at the time, but I noticed Noel had grown out of his boyish looks and was starting to appear more like a young teenager. His hair was a little longer than when he was at home. Noel seemed to be more mature and more respectful. But was he really? I would always go back home knowing I had lost him and things would never be the same as before. I spent many lonely nights crying about my loss and praying to God to bring him back home and to make him normal again.

Eventually, Noel was able to come home, and I thought it would be for good. I was so happy that God had answered my prayers. We were finally back together again! He was going into the ninth grade, and I was hitting my senior year. Noel was getting readapted to home again, and then, almost as soon as he arrived, the troubles began all over again. Noel was smoking by then, and I guess in a loving way, Dad Grant was giving him the smokes. Mom Grant nonetheless was afraid of him, and she was not going to let up on Dad until Noel was out of the house!

Over the years, our adoptive parents continued to love and take care of us kids. As we became teenagers, we began to feel we were in everyone's way and needed to remain to ourselves. We did not want to tell anyone how these awkward feelings were affecting us individually, as we feared possible rejection. Looking back, I really do not think our parents realized what we were feeling or the ever-growing disconnection between us. I think, too, this is a feeling most adopted children get during their lives at one point or another. Perhaps, as a result, these feelings come from not knowing our bio-parents or due to the disconnection from our siblings. Alternatively, perhaps it comes from reliving the rejection we previously endured in our lives. Foster care and adoption have a huge impact on children, especially if they are older. Sometimes this impact is physical and not just mental. I feel more mentally affected because of the many remaining unanswered questions.

Then a sad day came. Noel was taken to the Lena Pope home in Fort Worth. As Dad Grant took Noel to be admitted, he was in tears. For any parent, this is a heart-wrenching experience. We did not get to see Noel ever again. My heart dropped, and I felt responsible and at fault that he had to leave. It was very hard for me to accept his leaving once again. I felt as though Mom Grant had pushed a little too hard to get him out of the home and away from the family. However, from her viewpoint, it was understandable, as the family security had to be a priority.

Many years went by, and I wondered what happened to my Noel. We had such good times together. We were told he was very sick and needed to be left alone with the professionals. When would we ever get to see or hear from him again? Why could we not see or talk to him? Another part of my life was torn away, and the hurt just kept piling on. It was bad enough to lose my biological family—and now Noel. Would I lose contact with him just as I lost contact with my biological family? A great feeling of loneliness began to nag at me, and it was getting harder to accept.

Was Jesus just as lonely? I asked myself. *Did He too feel like everyone was against Him? Where were all of His siblings while growing up? Why doesn't the Bible give us more information on them?* Going through high school without Noel present took all of the fun out of it. It was then I had to learn to make as many friends as possible in order to hide the hurt and to focus on continuing with my education.

I will not leave you comfortless: I will come to you.
—John 14:18 (KJV)

The Fear of Going to Viet Nam
Ω

My senior year came in 1970 and went by in a hurry. I would go to school and get out around two each day. I had enough credits to leave early in order to drive to work in Irving for Dad Grant at his grocery store. His company, Big Value, was just getting started. It soon became a major supermarket competitor. Dad Grant had left Buddies Supermarkets along with a good friend, Walter, to start their business together. Dad Grant had been a vice president of the Grocery Department, and Walter was the vice president of the Meat Department. The two together became a powerful force against the competition.

I would drive to Irving every day to work until closing time and then return home to do homework until the wee hours in the morning. It was my goal to save as much money as possible. Grandad Johnson had sold me his white 1960 Chevy Impala for a thousand dollars, so it was imperative to pay him back. This was a major step up from the black and white bike I had in my early years.

However, looming in the back of my mind and every young man's mind in America at this time was the Viet Nam War. During my high school days, the daily news reported of how terrible the war had become with a high percentage of soldiers dying. The public was at odds as to the purpose and reasoning of America's involvement. I was a very confused young man when it came to my view of the war and our government's position on the matter. I was not mature enough to understand what it was all about and why the country was even involved. Each day my graduation day got a little closer, and I just knew my turn to be chosen for the draft lottery was also getting nearer. Was I to skip out and run to Canada like so many of my peers, or was I to let the government forces be in control and draft me into the army? On the other hand, was I to volunteer for one of the other branches of service and face the music? I weighed the pros and cons day after day. The closer it got to my graduation day, the more fear I developed. It was getting harder for me to concentrate on my studies, pondering and praying each day that God would help me to make the right decision. I just wanted to live and have a decent life ahead of me. I strongly believe in serving one's country, as it is always a person's duty to be patriotic and supportive. We were taught to serve God first and then country.

With great confidence, I knew that once my graduation day was over, my Selective Service number would be in the mail! It was my understanding the lower the number, the greater the chance of being inducted into the army. Then, "Hello, Viet Nam!" The odds of surviving Nam were slim for most, and with my kind of luck, I would be dead within the first week of setting foot on the enemy's soil. As the war continued, it proved to be a death wish, as the returning dead were tremendous. Many of my friends were terrified of going there!

Then one day before graduation, a good friend, Jay, told me to go with him and sign up for the air force. His dad, who was a retired colonel, said joining the air force would be the next best way to stay out of the trenches. We both figured it would be the safest bet, and we could join under the buddy system. In addition, we would earn points to help us go to college after a six-year commitment. Since Dad Grant repeatedly told me he absolutely would not pay for my college, joining the service would be the right decision to make.

Praise God for watching over and helping me to see the right path during this troubling time.

Jay and I faced the situation head-on and took the entrance exam at the federal offices in Dallas. Soon I received a notification advising me I had passed the entrance exam. It was then I told my parents of the decision to join the service. Mom Grant was so mad at me for joining the service, but she was mostly upset knowing the odds of survival. Dad Grant knew it was best for me to get out and move on with my life. He even drove me to the facility, said good-bye, and then hurriedly drove off. I could tell he was upset, and yet he knew it was the right decision. He had served in the army as an attachment to the Air Corps during the Korean conflict. He was glad to have made it home alive but knew I needed the experience as well. The military would help to make me stronger. It would teach me to be a man, and perhaps I could learn a trade.

It is horrific so many young men died in Viet Nam. It was even more devastating the number of soldiers that became hooked on drugs and suffered so needlessly upon their return home. No one liked the war. Worse yet, the American public ignored its returning soldiers. Because of the war, people on all sides of the confrontation became wounded both physically and mentally. The French left Viet Nam for a reason, and the United States should have learned from their lessons.

After graduation, my life changed very rapidly. Soon after receiving my acceptance letter, I was off to San Antonio for boot camp at Lackland AFB. Folks have always said, "When you send a boy to war, he will come back a man. Dead or alive!" I truly believe this with all of my heart. It was the most terrifying experience to leave home not knowing when I would return, or even if I stood a mere chance of survival. I prayed every night that God would direct me and keep me safe. Over the next several months, this insecure boy was shaped into a man. I had changed just as a caterpillar changes into a butterfly. I had left the security of my boyhood cocoon-like home and emerged into a different, more colorful being altogether. It was a mysterious but good change. I really did not miss the old me. In addition, I did not know where I was headed in life. However, I knew that God was in charge now. All I had to do was to listen to Him and pray often.

I spent the next six weeks in boot camp learning the basics of military life. The constant shooting, running, walking, running some more, exercising, and conditioning my puny little body from a ninety-pound, six-foot weakling into a 125-pound source of shear muscle and stamina. I was a sickly kid growing up and had all of the childhood illnesses that kept me puny. It was well worth the agonizing muscle pain to see my personal metamorphosis. The early morning exercises and the three square meals were the perfect program. Yet each day I was worried not about the day of graduating from boot camp but about what would happen afterward. What next? Where would I go? What would be my position? Would I live? Would I ever see my family and friends again? Would I ever get to see my younger brothers, Sid and Noel, again? Was all of the agonizing physical training and mental preparation going to go to waste on a deadly battlefield?

After successfully enduring the gruesome air force basic training, it was not long before I successfully graduated from boot camp. It was an exciting moment, but my family was not there, and I felt at a loss, as the excitement simply came and went. There were many people at the ceremony, but I was all alone. Holding back the tears, I simply walked off the parade field and went back to my barracks.

Thousands of troops had marched in their finest attire that day as the top brass looked on in review. The drill sergeants were screaming out their direct commands at the top of their lungs. The perfect formation of all of the marching units was amazing and sent goose bumps down my back. Moreover, as each unit marched by the review stand, a loud cheer would surge from the crowd. It was a day to remember! It was a day to be proud of our accomplishments and yet a somber day. Many of my friends would soon be leaving for a predetermined military destination, possibly Viet Nam. As anticipated, some would not return to their childhood homes.

I was glad this part of my military training was over, as I looked forward to leaving Lackland AFB and getting on with a new way of life. My fellow boot camp friends were all receiving their orders, and many were going to tech schools across the country before shipping out to wherever. I remained on base in a state of limbo known as "Casual Status." My new assignment involved cleaning toilets, picking up cigarette butts, and raking dirt. Oh for heaven's sake! It was my duty to serve my country while making sure the grounds were policed daily from 8:00 a.m. until 3:00 p.m.! *What a sheer waste of my talents,* I thought. *Why am I being punished this way?* No one could answer my questions or tell me why I was being singled out for such foolishness! Raking dirt! For Pete's sake. What was the point? To this day, I have somewhat of a grudge against smokers, as so many of them just throw their cigarette butts onto the ground. How rude. If you are going to smoke, please put the butts in the trash or in a coffee can and do not simply throw them down on the ground. I am tired of raking the dirt already! (I do have to admit the raked dirt pattern does look cool.)

On one ordinary and boring day, just after cleaning the headquarters' restrooms, I received a summons to appear before the Office of Special Investigations. (This is a military department very similar to the CIA.) What had I done to get such an invitation? Just to mention the initials of the OSI was frightening! This waiting period was long enough to give anyone a heart attack! I was certainly a nervous wreck while waiting for the big day. If only I had legal counsel to go with me. However, the only counselor I had was God, and He and I were not talking that day. I could have used a little screaming or a subtle conversation to calm me down. Hmmm.

I had to walk clear across to the far side of the base in order to attend the appointment. As per the orders received, I wore my 1505 semi-dress uniform. It is a khaki-colored uniform considered as casual dress and one step below the dress blues. My roll-on was beginning to roll off as I sat in the office in anticipation of finding out my fate. As I sat quietly, my mind was racing ahead. What could I possibly have done during my childhood that would have brought me to meet with the OSI? I did not cheat on any tests at school. Nor did I steal anything that I could remember. I had never intentionally fought with anyone other than my brother as we played Cowboys and Indians. What could it be?

Then the moment of greatest tension came. A senior airman escorted me toward a cluttered police-like office, and the door was quickly shut behind me. *Oh, God ... If you are anywhere right now, please be at my back, because I recognize this is not going to be good!*

After a few moments of chitchatting with the ranking detective behind the desk and getting to know him a little, I finally started to relax and settle down. The sweat that had been pouring down my back finally started to cease, and I was beginning to be a little chilled. It was then that I found out the air force wanted to train me to become a spy. *Do what? The OSI wants this four-eyed, scrawny, clown of a person to be a what? A spy?* In a movie perhaps but not for real! The officer explained that I had been subjected to an extensive background search over the last several weeks and was issued a top-secret clearance. They had already given me a code name and a secret job description. What did I get myself into this time?

A few days later, I finally received permission to call my parents to tell them I was going to be a non-Morse printer operator (whatever that was). They were relieved, but I was nervously concerned as to where I would be stationed next. I just kept asking myself if they even had non-Morse operators in Viet Nam. A spy? I just did not see myself as Agent 007. Lord, you really outdid yourself that time!

Eventually, my orders arrived, and I headed straight to San Angelo's Goodfellow Air Force Base. It was there I spent the next six weeks in an extensive training program learning about computers, electronics, a little Russian, and Morse code. I had never learned so much in such a little time. The air force has a special way of teaching things that no other institution has mastered. If you do not pass a course, you start over repeatedly until you learn it. Moreover, if you could not endure the pressure or pass the tests, it was off to the kitchen to peel potatoes! This is such a great way of beating things into your head. The technique works, and it is amazing how quickly the material is learned.

Goodfellow is a small base and was one of the loneliest places in the world to be stationed, especially during Christmas. San Angelo is very cold during the winter due to its southwest Texas location. I had never dreamed of a place being so cold, and it snowed a lot that year! I believe it was in October 1971. We not only had to go to school, but we also had guard duty. There is nothing lonelier than guarding a somewhat pitch-dark base during a long, cold night. Can you imagine just walking back and forth from one end of the base to the other from 11:00 p.m. until 7:00 a.m. in the cold, wet snow? You could hear the coyotes bawl for miles! You knew the likelihood of a Communist threat was almost nil, but any soldier sitting in the dark with an MK-16 was a perfect target for anything! Even for the aliens that would be creeping up on you as they waited for the right chance to gobble you up! Just like in the old black-and-white movies. It is amazing how your mind plays tricks on you while all alone in the dark. I could not wait for my relief to show up. Nothing like a hot cup of coffee and a good six hours of sleep to get back to normal.

Soon the technical training was over, and I had finally mastered my electronics and Morse code. I was a little fuzzy on the Russian, but I had learned enough to move on. I rather hated to leave Goodfellow, as it became a home for a while and I began to feel somewhat safe there (during the day). My next mission was down the road, and the next stop was at Keesler Air Force Base in Biloxi, Mississippi.

This was a much bigger base, and compared to Goodfellow AFB, it was like a giant city of its own. During the war, this base was busy with huge planes and jets coming and going constantly. Conveniently located at the Gulf of Mexico, it was easy to visit the beach. If anything, trees surrounded the base, and the climate was warm with occasional sea breezes. I had a great feeling about this base. It was different from most, and having local businesses in close proximity made the area feel more like home.

One day while I was in class trying to master Morse code with a typewriter, a couple of military policemen opened our classroom door to admit a new student. Lo and behold, guess who showed up! Do you remember reading earlier about my sign-up friend, Jay? Evidently, Jay had graduated from basic training as well. We had both been taking the same training path. He was just a few weeks ahead of me. I could not wait to find out the details.

I had the chance to walk across the base to go see him later that evening. Evidently, my high school friend had gone AWOL (absent without leave) and was caught somewhere off base. He had started drinking, smoking, and taking drugs, thus landing himself in jail for a while. The service introduced him back into the system as a second chance to clean up his act. I was so ashamed and very irritated with him. I could not understand why he made these choices, but according to him, it was all a game. Reluctantly, I made the decision not to associate with him anymore. I wished him the best of luck and said my good-byes with tears in my eyes. My high school friend had become an entirely different person.

A part of my childhood had just drifted further away. What next? What else from my past would go to the wayside? I had a sense of loneliness that evening and retired to my bunk with great sadness and more tears in my eyes. I had lost a very dear friend, and I could not help him. My hopes of our continued friendship became dismal, and his future was obviously going nowhere. According to 1 John 2:15–16 (KJV), the Bible speaks of lust of the flesh. "Love not the world, neither the things that are in the world. If any man love the world, the love of the Father is not in him. For all that is in the world, the lust of the flesh, and the lust of the eyes, and the pride of life, is not of the Father, but is of the world." James 1:14–15, KJV, reminds us, "But every man is tempted, when he is drawn away of his own lust, and enticed. Then when lust hath conceived, it bringeth forth sin: and sin, when it is finished, bringeth forth death."

It was my first Viet Nam tragedy. and it left me heart sickened, lonely, and with a great loss. Jay and I had done everything together. We took the same classes, ran the streets together, and supported each other. Miraculously, during another tragic moment later in my life, I was able to see him again.

While stationed at Keesler AFB, I received word from my commanding officer and the American Red Cross that Mom Grant had been admitted into a hospital. At the same time, my great-grandfather, Papa Shelley, was in the same hospital and was not expected to live. Papa Shelley was Dad Grant's grandfather on his mom's side of the family.

I was blessed to catch a flight home on such a short notice at the beginning of a Mother's Day weekend. Mom Grant was ill from pneumonia, but with the proper medication, she would get well soon. Unfortunately, Papa Shelley was not going to make it. I was able to hold his hand and tell him we were going fishing soon. (We had always joked about going together even though he was almost blind.) That got a smile from him as always. I knew he had held out as long as he was able. Papa Shelley had the most beautiful white hair and twinkling bold eyes that simply made me feel loved. He never said anything negative and was always good to me. The following day, our dear Papa Shelley passed away. I was not able to attend the funeral, as I had to be back at the base the same day. I was so glad to have had the opportunity to see his smile just one more time. It was so good to have held his hand and just to know he loved us all. I simply could not have handled a funeral at the time. I missed him deeply in my heart. I loved him so much.

My furlough was just long enough to see Mom Grant and make sure she was going to be okay. She hated to see me go but understood the situation and was glad I had come to see her. The excitement of seeing me in my uniform made her feel much better. Dad Grant was glad to see me too and noticed how much weight I had gained. He could not believe it was even me. I think the uniform made them proud, and they actually showed signs of missing me. Dad Grant hated to see me go. This time, he took a little more effort to tell me good-bye. As I flew out of the Great Southwest International Airport, I had a deep sadness in my heart and a lump in my throat. Would I be able to return home? *Jesus my Lord, what is next in my life and please do not leave me alone. I need you in my life as my Savior and protector.*

A uniform eventually changes a person. Sometimes it is for the better, and then again sometimes not so much. In my case, I felt respected for the first time in my life. It was heartbreaking that I had to leave home just to gain what I needed most in life. Perhaps the decision to join the air force was a good one. I knew then God was really taking care of me, and I knew this mini-break was what I needed. Despite the loss, I was so thankful for the experience and the respect I was finally gaining.

Soon it was time to transfer to another assignment. This time I had to leave the homeland for Karamursel, Turkey. It was as though I was getting further and further away from home with every new set of orders. Half a world away, my new home would be at an underground defense base off the coast of the Sea of Marmara. I had not been trained to speak Turkish, so why was I studying the Russian lessons back at Goodfellow?

Slowly, I was learning how to fend for myself. Traveling to a foreign country for the first time was enough to send fear throughout my body. In confidence, I remembered the touch of God from years before and knew He was at my side. *Just let Him guide you,* I kept reminding myself. My catechism classes taught me to let God show me the way, for He is the Good Shepherd that will watch over me. This reminds me of Psalm 121:7, "The Lord shall preserve thee from all evil; he shall preserve thy soul" (KJV).

This was the most frightening journey up to this point in my life. It involved several hours of flying from Fort Worth to Kennedy International in New York, to London, to Rheine Mein, and then finally to Istanbul. (Istanbul is the modern name for Constantinople.) Armed with my duffle bag and my Bible, the Pan Am 747 jet finally landed in the middle of nowhere on Turkish soil. The plane's crew and passengers were unloaded immediately outside the plane. Quickly, a group of Turkish soldiers toting machine guns surrounded the group. This was a very impressive greeting, I might add! We were loaded into awaiting buses and driven to a very large open-air, metal-roofed, barnlike building for what I believed to be Turkish Interrogation 101.

All of the foreign passengers, including myself, felt pure fear in every respect. The only English-speaking military companion I knew was a person from Indiana whom I had met on the plane. Little did I know Joe would become one of my best friends ever! To this day, we are godparents to each other's kids. We both feared for our lives and had no clue what was going to happen to any one of us. Strategically, we took our military training into action. We knew sticking close to each other would be our safest chance of survival! There is nothing like a mutual bonding that matures into a lifelong friendship. Was this God's way of replacing my old friend Jay?

A few minutes after arriving at the "cattle corrals," one of the guards shouted out in English for us to lay our bags onto the long metal conveyors and to step aside. "Don't go anywhere and don't grab your bag until you are told to do so!" demanded the guards. Shortly after that, a young civilian started to run toward the corralled passengers yelling at us to stay together. He identified himself as a US liaison and said we were to follow his instructions. In my mind: *Yeah right ... show me your credentials!*

Then I noticed he was talking to a few of the Turkish guards about our bags and told them to move all of the military bags into one specific area. It was then I noticed many of the passengers from the flight were actually US military troops, and some of these had their families with them. I was questioning myself as to who in their right mind would bring their family into this country. It was so obvious this country was not a safe place to vacation or visit with the family. I thought to myself, *Is this it? Rather than in Viet Nam, is this where I am killed or kidnapped?* I spent the next few minutes trying to scan the area to see if we were really in some kind of danger. *Lord, are you here? Do you have my back?* Deuteronomy 31:6 teaches us to be strong and courageous and not to be afraid, for the Lord our God goes with us and will never leave or forsake us. Yes, God had my back, no doubt about it.

Joe and I stuck together like glue. The airport attendees moved our luggage to the end of long metal conveyor. Finally, we were quickly loaded into an awaiting bus along with our luggage. I had noticed the blue air force color and the yellow USAF markings on the side. It was either official or an excellent replica. It had been an hour or so of getting our luggage loaded into this bus. Then finally the doors were shut and we were off to what we thought would be a short ride to the base. If the trip were to be only a short drive, we would be settling in for the night before long. We were all so tired and hungry after the long flight and airport greeting. The scary ordeal at the baggage checkpoint took a lot of life out of us as well. Little did we realize our journey ahead would be six hours or more, and we would be on one of the most dangerous highways in the world!

The bus driver took us from Istanbul across the historical Galata Bridge to the Asian side of Turkey. The direction took us into the mountains and then ran along the east shore of the Sea of Marmara. The primitive highway was barely one lane wide. The rule of thumb in Turkey is the largest vehicle on the road has the right of way!

Can you imagine a bus driver speeding sixty to seventy miles an hour on a treacherous highway, high up in the mountains, leaning out the driver's window while shouting at an oncoming diesel truck twice the size of the bus? Talk about fear! Talk about wanting to get out and walk! Talk about closing your eyes and praying to God that you will get to wherever you are going in once piece, let alone alive! The custom was definitely a strange one, and every Turk will tell you they believe in fate. If they should die while hanging out that window, so be it.

Several hours later, we arrived at the base with very little life left within us. It was very dark outside, and not to our surprise, Turkish Naval guards met us at the gate. They boarded and inspected the bus inside and out, and then they allowed us to move forward and out of the bus. The Turks separated us into two groups ... single troops and married soldiers with families. In my mind, this could not be good.

They lined us up and indicated for us to march forward without our bags, as these were to remain at the gate. We were directed into a large building that served as a mess hall. Finally, we had a sense of relief and something to eat! A group of US soldiers fed us "Beanie Weenies" and served soft-serve ice cream. I was so tired that I did not feel like eating, but the US soldiers attending to us insisted we should eat because of our low energy levels. It tasted so good, but all I wanted was to sleep. Sleep deprivation can lead to serious consequences and even death.

An American officer entered the mess hall to give us a formal greeting. He apologized for the semi-hostile environment. He hoped we were all okay and insisted we eat plenty but not take too long. He said we would most likely sleep for several hours due to the trauma we endured during the day. We were to report in two days to the base headquarters across the way from the mess hall where we were presently eating.

After completing our meals, we were led back to our bags and then escorted to a designated dormitory-like facility for incoming single troops and another one for soldiers with families. We were given directions to our rooms after receiving the assigned keys to our rooms. I was going to be sharing a room with another soldier who was already fast asleep. I did my best not to wake him as I crawled into the usual military bunk while keeping the lights out. Good thing I had my official dark green military-issued flashlight with both a clear and red lens. The red lens kept the bright light subdued, but I could still see well enough to get around in the room.

It seemed like an eternity since I had left Texas, and it was good to finally crawl into a bed. I remember my downtime was about fourteen hours from that moment. I could not wait for daylight to find out where in this world I had landed. When I finally awoke, I could not tell you if it was morning or evening. I found someone walking in a hallway to ask what time it was, and he said it was evening with a puzzled look on his face. I explained my arrival from the day before and my unusual disorientated feeling. Laughing, he agreed it would take a couple of days to regain my frame of mind. I had until the next morning to check in at headquarters. Feeling a little ill, I just lay back down and slept some more. Nothing like enduring jet lag, which offers a delusional and uncomfortable feeling for at least a couple of days. It is written in Matthew 11:28

(KJV) where Jesus said, "Come unto me, all ye that labour and are heavy laden, and I will give you rest." And rest, I did!

It was not long before I became accustomed to the lifestyle of a soldier in a foreign country. The flights (air force groups) were subdivided into four groups—Alpha, Baker, Charlie, and Dog flights. I had been assigned to the Charlie Flight and soon began learning all I could about the country, the base, and the job. I made good friends and even began to venture out with them on a few excursions. Learning the language was a little difficult at first, but learning how not to be ripped off was even harder. There were numerous gypsy workers living near the base, so we were advised to keep our belongings locked up. I was very fortunate no one ever bothered my personal items. I did see the gypsies rummaging through the dumpsters occasionally for items that might be of some use. It was so sad to see such poverty among us. If only there were a program or something to help them. Since the US military was a guest in the country, there was little we could do as the result of the Turkish laws and restrictions in place.

Turkey is a beautiful country around the size of Texas. There is no wondering as to why this part of the world became such a major concern for so many civilizations. It is diverse, it is unique, and it is intriguing. In 1971, Turkey was still a somewhat young country still learning the basics of engineering, the science of electronics, and similar modern industries that the larger countries were already mastering. This is why the country still had its mystical charm. The beauty of the Blue Mosque and other ancient buildings majestically lure tourists to her charm. The countryside embraces small enchanting villages to historical civilizations once feared. In addition, Ankara, the capital located on the Asian side of the country, proudly displays its modern flare. There is such a wide range of interests from the seaside villages with plenty of fishing boats to the ski slopes of snow-covered mountains. Turkey is simply one of the world's best tourist destinations.

What I loved most about Turkey were its ancient sites, including the Seven Churches of Asia Minor! Traveling within the country is very economical, and should anyone desire to take a trip within the country, the *dolmus*—a Turkish minibus or taxi, pronounced dole-moosh—is the best way to go anywhere within the country, providing it is not going into the mountains! Alternatively, try your fancy on a camel!

I think God really wanted me to go to Turkey because He wanted me to learn more about my Christian faith. I also needed to learn about the diversity of other religions as well as how to survive in a foreign environment. The next two years of my life changed me dramatically. I received an education not only from my military duties but also from the traveling, and I took it to heart. Bonding with the local people from across Turkey and Europe was the best gift that God could have ever given me. At times, it felt that I was dreaming, and every day I would wake up to a new story. New adventures ... some not so inviting as others but a challenge, to learn and to develop my inner self.

> When I was a child, I spake as a child, I understood as a child, I thought as a child: but when I became a man, I put away childish things.
> —1 Corinthians 13:11 (KJV)

A Soldier's Mail

Ω

E ven though I was overseas for what seemed a long time, I
continued to miss my family and friends at home. I tried so hard
not to let the slowly passing days, weeks, and months bother me
mentally. Had it not been for the almost weekly letters from my best
friend, Charlene, her parents, and my parents, I do not think I could
have endured the loneliness that every soldier dreads. Thank God I
received letters from someone almost every other week! I would go
into a deep depression when I did not get a letter from them.

Mail call is a GI's best friend, and when nothing arrives, it
becomes a depressing communications disconnect until the next
mail call. Many of us would share our letters with one another
and would read them repeatedly to help pass the time. Television,
radio, and tape cassettes were not an option for entertainment. On
occasion, records would arrive at the BX. We would take turns
buying them. Not everyone had a record player. It was great to
listen to records with our friends who had the players. During our
time off, several friends would get together and play our records
for hours.

During my senior year in high school, in 1970, I had met Charlene
Lauderdale at Dad Grant's grocery store in Irving, Texas. She was a
young beauty of a cashier that I secretly admired. I had nothing to
do with her though, because I felt so inferior and not good enough

for such a fancy. All of the other stock boys would hang out with her, and it made me feel so left out. Besides, I had to concentrate on the war and my future. I did not want to be attached to anyone, just in case I did not make it back home. What a wimp I was indeed. A four-eyed, ninety-pound nerd of a person.

One day I had the opportunity to carry groceries to her parents' car. Her mom and dad were nice to me. I heard her mom say, "Charlene, he is such a nice young man. You should marry him some day." Charlene replied, "Oh, Momma, that is the boss's son. I don't ever see marrying him." Little did either of us know how our lives would change down the road! God had plans for each of us, and it was totally a shocker!

I did however get up enough gumption to ask Charlene to write me, since I felt that she really would. I was delighted that she had agreed and that she would miss me as well. I even made an agreement to sell my Impala to her best friend, Paul. Selling that old Impala was like losing my closest friend. As a result, I eventually gained a better friend because of the deal.

One lonely day, I realized Charlene had not written me for several weeks. The stories I told myself were getting the best of me. I would question myself. *What if I wrote something to make her angry with me? What if she is ill or moved far away, somewhere unknown? Even worse, what if she got married? Surely, she would have told me. Or would she?*

I sat down in a panic and wrote a letter to her mom, apologizing for the intrusion of her privacy, but I needed to understand what happened to Charlene. Her mom eventually wrote me back, and I was surprised to discover that Charlene had moved to her cousin's in St. Joseph, Missouri. She had taken a job at the Whitaker Cable Company assembling auto cables for Chrysler. Her parents had expected her return home soon, but her mom was not certain of Charlene's personal plans at the time.

Upon getting the encouraging good news, I immediately wrote Charlene a letter. Somehow, I got up the courage to tell her how much I really appreciated her writing me and really felt compelled to marry her. Then I went on to say how I was really discouraged not getting a letter from her over the past several weeks. I poured out my feelings and then mailed it off with such haste. After mailing it, I became a real nutcase. I was so ashamed of my actions and felt her loss of friendship forever. My mental state was so bad that I tried drinking two beers a week with ice cream in order to drown my sorrow! Such a sad case!

My friend Joe tried to get me back on track by luring me off base to visit a couple of friends' apartment in Yalova. This married couple was also in the air force, and they were his good friends. Surely as a married couple they would understand my predicament. They understood all right ... enough to get me unintentionally sauced on a special orange juice known as Harvey Wall Bangers to ease my pain and suffering! I will never drink anything that strong again! The morning after, with constant nausea and vomiting, was just too much for this love-sickened soldier. Even though I had been tricked, we are still good friends. At the time, I was not aware that I am allergic to orange juice!

Several weeks went by without letters, and then finally the delivery of all mail calls! A letter from Charlene. I was so happy I began to cry, and I had not even opened the letter! The always-perfumed envelope sent a soothing aroma to my brain and eased my tensions. Yet I was fearing the letter might contain the bad news I was dreading so much. Then the guilt stories in my head started to come and haunt me again. After what seemed to be an eternity, I nervously began to open the letter. Was this the much-dreaded soldier's ill fate of not getting future mail from that one special person?

Slowly, I began to read all about how she was very sorry for not writing sooner. She had been caught up in the excitement of moving to St. Jo and having fun with her cousins. Charlene had reached the legal drinking age, and it was time to party, to get a job, to go motorcycle riding, and simply enjoy the grand time of things. Life was being good to her.

Then the dreaded news! She had written that under no circumstances would she marry me, but she would continue to write. Finally, I thought, the guarantee I needed to hear ... she would continue to write. That marriage thing ... it could wait. At least I would be in contact with her, and a second chance would come eventually. My day to ask her again would come. I just knew it! In the meantime, I had her letters coming and that wonderful aroma to help me keep my sanity. Thank God for Charlene!

I had the opportunity to travel to Salzburg, Austria, and decided to send her a small token of my appreciation for writing. Mom Grant had always taught us boys to be very appreciative of the nice things people do for us. Therefore, I took the liberty to buy a tiny blue crystal elephant and mailed it to Charlene. It was so tiny I had to pack it in a slightly large box so shipping it would not be an issue. (Besides, trying to travel incognito with a large gift-wrapped package would blow my cover.) I was able to hide the tiny gift in my boot for safe travel back to the base.

When Charlene received the package, her cousins had her convinced the package contained an engagement ring. Charlene was so mad that she refused to open the dainty box and left it on the kitchen countertop for days. Scolding her for not opening the box, the cousins said it was wrong to keep me waiting, if indeed the box contained an engagement ring. The cousins finally encouraged Charlene to open the box. They said I deserved an answer one way or another.

Finally, she reluctantly opened the box. I understand it was quite an amusement to see the look on her face when the very small, blue Austrian crystal elephant revealed itself! Not the ring she was really expecting! *Ha! Ha!* Her cousins had a field day laughing and rolling on the floor! Charlene was so mad at them for poking so much fun at her after the great reveal! In fact, she was actually upset at me in her mind, but in her heart, she was relieved. Only to a small degree though, as her cousins said she showed some signs of disappointment.

> Delight thyself also in the Lord; and he shall
> give thee the desires of thine heart.
> —Psalm 37:4 (KJV)

A Step toward Death

Ω

One day Joe and I had decided to get off the base for a while in order to get some duly deserved rest and relaxation. We knew it would be easy to catch a dolmus to the city of Bursa. Folks were telling us about a great ski resort on top of Uludag Mountain. Joe thought it would be the perfect spot to take pictures, as he and I were big into developing our own film. It seemed like a great idea at the time.

The nearer we got to Bursa, the worse the idea became. It had snowed a lot during the week, so we expected the mountain to have some coverage. Finally we reached our destination and were surprised Uludag was heavily blanketed with a deep layer of snow. However, we had become such adventurous soldiers, and any amount of snow was not going to stop our plans to go to the top!

After arriving in Bursa, we hired a cab driver who managed to take us almost to the top near the resort. To our dismay, the snow was much deeper than what we had expected. The ski lodge was closed, and it was obvious why. The snow covered all four sides of the building and most of the roof. I do not think anyone could get into the lodge even if the snow melted for months!

After a taking a few awesome pictures of the scenery and the blanketed lodge, we decided it was best to head back down the mountain before it became too dark to see our way. I did not like traveling too far from the base at night because it was so hard to find our way back, let alone understand the foreign signs. Besides, the cab driver was faithfully waiting, and we certainly did not want him to take off without us! That would be a long, treacherous walk back down the mountain, let alone trying to get back to Bursa. Not a good thought.

Joe was about twenty feet ahead of me as we were heading back down the mountain slope toward the awaiting taxi. We were making good timing when the death trap opened up. I suddenly fell into a bottomless hole with my arms stretched out, holding me in place for dear life! "Joe! Joe!" I screamed to the top of my lungs. "Joe! Joe!" I tried not to move, as I did not want the snow to give way to my weight or movements. Just one wrong move, and I was surely a dead man!

Joe finally heard my screaming and turned around in disbelief. He immediately ran back to see what was happening. I told him to be careful and not to come too close. He stopped suddenly, surveyed the situation, and in a shear panic grabbed my hand and pulled me out in a split second! With extreme adrenaline, he had amazing strength to yank me out of that hole with just one quick jerk! Thank God, Joe heard my screaming! My life was flashing before me, and my heart was throbbing at ninety beats a second! Afterward, I kept asking myself why Joe did not fall into the hole. Just a few seconds before me, he had taken the same exact path. I do not think I would have had the strength to pull him out had he fallen into the bottomless pit. Joe was much taller and stronger than I was. We would have both wound up in the hole and gone forever if I had been the one doing the pulling!

I prayed to God to get us safely down the mountain and back to the base. I barely escaped death that day and stayed awake for several nights pondering over the incident. My Savior had protected both of us and had given Joe the strength to get me out without losing his grip on my hands. To this day, I remember the fear in my heart, and I am so thankful Joe was with me at the time. We never went back to the lodge to relocate the area of the incident. I continue to wonder about that hole and if it remains a danger.

One would think we learned our lesson about traveling in a foreign country without a guide. Nope. We decided to try our luck on a weekend excursion to Istanbul to see a local friend. During our trip, a group of young kids surrounded Joe when my back was turned. Either they were a gang getting ready to steal something from him or they were just going to pick on him. Something told me to turnaround—and quick! I knew right then that something was going to happen. Immediately, I started looking around for the police. When I started screaming for them, the kids took off running, leaving Joe safely behind. A couple of police did eventually arrive, and we reported the incident. This was another one of those weird days. Satan, the enemy, just seemed to test our every move. He is always trying to get the best of every situation just for his benefit or laughter!

We never went out again on an excursion without the other one staying close by. We learned a powerful lesson that day, and we thanked God for watching over us. It was twice in just a few weeks that temptation was trying to do us in.

Sometimes God uses foolish things or events to give us a wakeup call or to complete His purpose. How often have we been in strange places or situations and asked God, "Why am I here?" Then, several years later while on the road of life, we find the true significance, reasoning, and the purpose of our former journey. The disciple Paul writes in 1 Corinthians 1:26–27: "For ye see your calling, brethren, how that not many wise men after the flesh, not many mighty, not many noble, are called: But God hath chosen the foolish things of the world to confound the wise; and God hath chosen the weak things of the world to confound the things which are mighty" (KJV). How wonderful are the mysteries of God!

Submit yourselves therefore to God. Resist
the devil, and he will flee from you.
—James 4:7 (KJV)

Returning Home to America
Ω

Several months before leaving Turkey, a special work event occurred. I remember working a lonely and cold graveyard shift in February 1972. It was one of those slow nights when trying to stay awake became a major challenge, but good hot coffee kept me going until the morning shift. As I was scanning various radio and other transmission frequencies, I suddenly heard an odd transmission that included Morse code. I quickly began confirmation of the location of the two parties transmitting the signals. A naval radar operator confirmed the signals were coming out of Bonn and Berlin. Our intelligence team received many briefings concerning this very secretive Bonn and Berlin radio, Morse code, and computer transmission. In the past, our interception of this communication was unsuccessful, as numerous previous operators simply could not keep up with the transcribing of the transmitted code. Normally the code would be followed by multiple frequency changes that occurred just before a sudden burst of computerized data. The Germans at this time had one of the fastest computer systems in the world.

Interception of this German transmission, in its entirety, would enable our country and NATO to gather super intelligence communicated between Berlin and Bonn. Knowing the diverse political cultures of both countries, this was a very important matter of interest to the free world. What were the two rivals so secretively transmitting? Whatever they were communicating certainly caught the attention of the intelligence world. Before my arrival to Turkey, this exchange was coming at least monthly over a very fast and powerful system. The free world wanted to get that intelligence at all costs. Even so, the United States had spent millions in resources to develop systems to break the ingenious German connection. Were these sensitive transmissions communicating plans to reunite the two powers? Were they sharing military or financial information? Were they discussing the possibility of tearing down the Berlin wall that eventually shocked the world in November 1989? After all, the Quadripartite Agreement of 1971 was allowing more East Germans to cross over for visitations into West Berlin and vice versa. However, the glorious reality of seeing two deeply rooted peoples coming back together after so many years of suffering would be an absolute miracle in itself! So many answered prayers!

God used me that night to help the free world discover whatever the Germans were discussing, and for that, I am so deeply proud and honored. My "super" ears and military training had finally paid off. I chased the signals across several different frequencies and quickly recorded the Morse code while frantically trying to keep up. Then it happened—a sudden burst of solid state-of-the-art German computer transmission! I had never seen anything like it before! This computerized transmission was so fast the printers I had previously set up to convert the German dialogue into English were sailing across the computer paper without stopping. At the end of the transmission, there must have been at least a thousand sheets of continuous dialogue.

Later that month, the intelligence analysts confirmed I had made a super military achievement. I had been able to intercept the whole transmission between Bonn and Berlin for the first time since the connection had been given top priority. The intelligence analysts were ecstatic! I still have the military certificates earned for this great achievement. Do you remember President Reagan's famous 1987 speech? "Mr. Gorbachev, tear down this wall!"

The fear of arriving in Istanbul months earlier finally disappeared from my pounding chest after a few days of getting used to the wonderful people of this remarkable host country. I had learned from my traveling experiences the best way to get back to the Istanbul airport was to take the ferry from the seaside town of Yalova. Many travelers would take this ferry to the Princess Islands, and then it would arrive at the Galata Bridge where a dolmus or a cab could be hired to get to the airport. This was a very quick journey of about one and half hours on the ferry across the Sea of Marmara. A very pleasant trip if one ignored the chicken and goat smells that diluted the splendor of hot chi (tea) and cheese sandwiches. This wonderful-tasting cheese is created using goats' milk and a delicate, manual curing process. However, it requires a few bites to begin enjoying its unique flavor. Anyone and his or her livestock could ride aboard the ferry, as this was a major transportation route for commerce and pleasure. Most travelers ride on the upper floor of the ferry to have a pleasant experience indeed!

After eighteen months in Turkey, my tour of duty was ending during the summer of 1973. Now a new anxiety developed as equally traumatic but for a different reason. I was saddened to leave my military friends at the base and those special citizens with whom I had bonded. I would be leaving the delightful residents living in Karamursel, Yalova, and Istanbul. These friendships were God-chosen for me and deeply touched my heart. Nevertheless, I had orders to move on, and there was no choice but to go. These memories and friendships will last forever in my heart and mind. Every now and then, I rekindle those special moments when I look at the thousands of pictures and slides I took during the few months I lived in this wonderful country.

The counting down of months, then weeks, and finally days to going home led to the number zero, the day of departure. It was time to go home to see family, to get back to Charlene, and once again to see America! There is no feeling greater to any soldier than that of day zero. It is in the hearts of every service man and woman that has been away from home for any length of time, especially after being on a dangerous assignment overseas.

I was so worried the plane would not land to take me home, or perhaps my ticket would be stolen or lost, or something would happen to prevent my getting on that plane. It seemed like an eternity before I finally boarded the big bird and landed in New York. My flight information was all misconstrued, and I landed on the wrong day, at the wrong time as had previously been determined. I called Dad Grant from the John F. Kennedy International Airport to advise it would be several hours into the night before I landed at Great Southwest International Airport in Fort Worth. Little did I know a welcome home party was planned for my return, but I missed the event by just a few hours. It was around two or three in the morning when Dad picked me up. I was severely exhausted from the extensive flight from Turkey, and I was very confused and lost yet in awe of the new surroundings and modernizations.

It was amazing how much lighting and new construction changed over the past eighteen months while I was away from home. New highways were completed, new buildings and ultra-tall pole lights lined the roads, and strange signs led the way home. There was so much contrast between the huge, well-lit American cities and the small, dark Turkish villages with little or no electric power. I had no recollection of the current surroundings and felt so deeply lost and out of place. *Was I really home?*

After a few minutes of saying my hellos to the immediate family, it was off to bed. While in Turkey, my adopted parents had moved from my childhood home to a much bigger two-story house. Sleeping under the new roof in an unfamiliar hotel-like room caught me weirdly off guard. Nevertheless, it did not matter now. All I wanted to do was sleep. And sleep I did. It must have been late the next evening before I finally eased out of bed and walked downstairs to see if anyone was around. Mom Grant was busy in the kitchen as I made my way wearily to the dining table. She was so astonished at how long I had slept and did not want the family to interrupt my rest.

The next few days were a new chapter in my life. I was trying my best to put together my past as a boy. Where were my old toys, my old clothes, and my younger days? Everything I could remember was gone. The move to the new residence resulted in almost complete eradication of my past. I was saddened over the loss of my boyhood stuff, as it was like losing a part of my childhood identity. Most of my past was gone, and only the memories now remained.

Losing my childhood possessions was probably meant to be, but I never really got over the loss. God had better plans, and crying over the lost possessions was not going to get me on the path of growing up and getting wiser. Better yet, the one thing I still had within my reach was the telephone number to a sweet little girl I once left behind. It was time to give her a visit. God was telling me to call Charlene and go see her. She was constantly on my mind. The challenge was to see if my adoptive parents would let me borrow a car to go see my letter-writing friend. God came through one more time and answered my prayers.

> For it is God which worketh in you both to
> will and to do of his good pleasure.
> —Philippians 2:13 (KJV)

From Letters to Love
Ω

I had this urgent need to see dear, sweet Charlene. Everyone just thought I was being premature. Dad Grant knew a little about Charlene, as she had worked for him in his Irving grocery store. He knew of her folks, and at this point Mom Grant had met Charlene a few times at the store but had never met her family. I tried my best to explain to Mom Grant how much I appreciated the fact Charlene had written to me devotedly; she was the only true friend remaining from my school days who had actually stayed in contact with me. The least I could do was take her out to eat just as a thank you for being so kind. Mom Grant agreed. Then, like a nervous teenager, I called Charlene. Just like a teasing girl, she would only accept my offer to go out if I would agree to wear my dress uniform! I do not think there is a red-blooded American boy who wants to wear a uniform after being glued to the thing for the previous two years! However, I reluctantly agreed, especially if it meant seeing her one more time before leaving for the Philippine Islands in a few short weeks.

The next step was to find a venue or some place to take this fine lassie and really impress her. Mom Grant suggested a dinner with a play at the now defunct Windmill Dinner Theater in Fort Worth. I had never heard of it, but she insisted it would be the place to go, and Charlene could dress up to feel special. The play title was *In One Bed and out the Other!* Oh no! This would be trouble in paradise if it were not a G rating. I could just hear Mrs. Lauderdale saying, "No … no! Absolutely not! You are not taking my daughter to a sleazy joint and definitely not to see an X-rated showing!"

It took some effort, but Mom Grant finally convinced Mrs. Lauderdale that it was not that kind of place and the on-stage drama was very G rated and funny. It would be the perfect place for us kids and our "date" that was not a date.

The big day finally came, and Dad Grant lent me his rusty old cream-colored Chrysler. It was not going to be the best showing of class in town, but at least I had a set of wheels to get me to and back from Irving. I was still not familiar with the new highways and traffic signs. Everything had changed so much over the years. As long as I continued east from Richland Hills, I was bound to run into a familiar traffic sign somewhere.

Deep inside my gut, at twenty years of age, I suddenly felt that teenage boy anxiety as I walked up to the Lauderdales' front door. I arrived early, so there was enough time to sit down and visit with Charlene and her family before taking off for the dinner theater. Charlene came to the door. Oh wow! She was all decked out in a burgundy, long dress with a ruffled neck collar and long sleeves. Her hair was long, naturally curly, and auburn. She had gleaming blue eyes, so beautiful, and was absolutely drop-dead gorgeous. I felt as though I was seeing a movie star! If only I had remembered to bring flowers! How clumsy of me to forget. It was a moment of happiness that I would never forget.

We walked into the front room, and all of her family was sitting around drinking coffee and talking about whatever came to mind. I could tell Charlene was on cloud nine, as she had not seen me for so long, and the uniform just lit up her face. She and I sat down on the couch together and talked a few minutes with her parents and family. Her daddy was just beaming, and her mom was talking a mile a minute. I could tell they were all a little nervous, so I thought it was best to get on the road. Knowing the drive back would be a challenge, I did not want to get lost. I had not been to this theater before, so finding it might be a little embarrassing.

We said our good-byes and headed out the door for the journey toward Cowtown. The trip to the theater did not take long, especially since I had a pretty lassie keeping me company. She seemed to be very interested in my military past and was excited about going out to eat and to the event. We had a lot to talk about, and the evening conversation brought back the old days at the grocery store.

Charlene's family had been through many tragic events over the years and had settled into their new home a few years prior. They were all from Wichita, Kansas, and had endured their share of home fires, tornadoes, flooding, and poverty. Her dad had managed to get a good position with LTV as a mechanic. The company at the time was a major aircraft and missile technology provider and was a major employer in the area.

The dinner and theater were great! We laughed our heads off and ate a wonderful meal, just as expected. I was so glad we attended the event, as it gave us both a chance to talk about the old days and what we had been doing over the last few years. With every glimpse of Charlene, this homesick soldier boy became more in love, and I knew this girl was the answer to my dreams. She was everything I remembered prior to going into the service, and she was just as bubbly and feisty as ever. I needed her in my life because she made me feel proud and wanted.

The night came closer to an end than anticipated, and we had a long trip back to Irving. I was able to extend my visit with Charlene's family and talk about the dinner, the play, and just about everything else that came to the conversation. It was getting very late, and finding my way back home in the dark would be a challenge, as the surroundings were not easily familiar.

Nervous as I was, I managed to get permission for a second date before leaving for the Philippines. It was a great evening watching the movie *Romeo and Juliet*. After this date, I knew deep down inside I did not want to lose Charlene. She was definitely the one I wanted to be with forever. Moreover, if taking her to the Philippines were an option, it would happen.

As the end of my leave drew closer, I managed to borrow Dad Grant's car one more time. Charlene and I were going to the local Pizza Hut for our final date. However, this time was going to be my last eye-to-eye contact with her for a while. I had to make a serious and life-changing decision.

I picked up Charlene, and we made our way to the Pizza Hut not far from her home. It was the best place to grab a salad and a great pizza. We ordered our meal, and every bite I took seemed to take forever to go down. Then finally I managed to ask her, "What do you think about long engagements?" She was a little startled by the question, let alone my unexpected approach.

I was a little confused myself but readdressed the upcoming tour of duty in the Philippines. By asking for a long-term engagement, I wanted to see if our long-distance relationship could grow. The way I saw it, an engagement before leaving again would be more mentally satisfying. I just wanted Charlene to be comfortable with the idea. To my surprise, she accepted the proposal! We agreed that if the long-distance engagement did not last, there would be no ill feelings between us. Nevertheless, once I returned home for good, we could give a real engagement a shot. After the big question, I started to relax, and the pizza started to go down a little easier. We had just agreed to be semi-engaged, and the next big step was to tell her parents. *Gulp! What have I done?*

Later in the evening, we gave the big news to Charlene's parents. I had asked her dad if he would accept the proposal, and he was thrilled. In fact, he was so happy tears started running down his face, and he was already calling me "son." A simple word I had not heard in many years. I had found an extended family that would love me as is. They did not care that I grew up as an adoptee; they saw past my personal poor financial status and accepted my rearing and education. Awesome!

Getting past this initial step was a great relief, as it was something that had bothered me frequently. I guess every young male goes through this process of trying to find that special person in his life. I know that I worried about with whom I would connect and what kind of family this soul mate would have. I was not certain if I had the qualifications to be marrying material. Nor did I think I had the personality and training to start a family of my own.

I relayed the news to Mom and Dad Grant; they were a little concerned and did not say much about it at the time. I did not get the feeling that they were totally on board with my decision, but it was my life, and for heaven's sake, I was twenty years old! Certainly I was old enough to start making my own decisions, good or bad. I knew God was in control, and He was coaching me all the way. I wanted to do His will and wanted to share my life with Charlene. God knew it, and He wanted me to be happy as well.

Even though I was excited about the new life ahead, I was blinded and did not know what was about to take place in the near future. However, behind my back, Satan was at work again trying to destroy what little joy I had recently received. Just like Job in the Bible, my faith was going to be seriously tested going forward. The next oversees trip would turn out to be an unforgettable walk toward death that unexpectedly came knocking at my door.

> Whoso findeth a wife findeth a good thing,
> and obtaineth favour of the LORD.
> —Proverbs 18:22 (KJV)

A Journey toward Death

Ω

I went one more time to see Charlene and say good-bye just before having to leave for the Philippines. It was a sad moment, but then again, it was with great joy, as I knew within a few months I would be returning home. It was this joyous thought I kept in my mind thereafter. Then the counting of the months, the days, and the hours started all over again—the soldier's dance. The countdown to zero. Once again the loneliness started, but at least this time I knew Charlene would be there waiting for me. Thank God for giving her to me! I can imagine how Adam felt before Eve was created. God knew man needed a companion. How wonderful that God loved Adam so much He gave him such a wonderful companion for a lifetime.

The fall of 1973 gave way to a long trip to the Philippines that began by leaving Oakland, California, on a TWA jet to Honolulu. It was a long flight, and midway one of the engines failed. Blessed once again, we made it to the airport without incident. There was a brief layover as another jet was prepared for the additional flight to Guam. I did not get to see much of Hawaii other than the beautifully decorated airport. It was just like a tropical paradise with all of the native plants and running water fountains, strategically placed to make any traveler at ease. It would have been nice to layover about two days so I could have seen more of the islands. Nevertheless, forces were at work to get all of the passengers back on track and in the air again.

It felt as though flying toward Guam I was going back in time, and history was repeating itself. I was getting very tired from the lack of sleep, just as during the flight when going to Turkey. However, this time the sun stayed blazing hot in the sky. I could not stop thinking about Charlene. Seeing her had been a blessing, and I just knew we were meant for each other. I kept laughing to myself about the day her mom had mentioned to Charlene that she should marry me, as I was a "nice" boy. Charlene and I had never dreamed her words would happen. Only God knew the unexpected comment would soon become a wonderful reality.

After several hours in the air, the flight finally landed in Guam. I was not certain where on the globe I was situated, but I knew it was near the far distant part of the world somewhere in the Pacific Ocean, a "billion" miles from the United States. There was a brief layover in Guam, just long enough to stretch our legs and to re-board the plane for the last stretch of ocean views. I did not know at the time that I had a biological uncle, George, living in Guam with his family. If only I knew Uncle George was in Guam, I could have called him. Perhaps I could have met with him and shared stories of the homeland. George was a carpenter by trade and completed many projects for the military on the island. (I was able to call him many years later, and he passed away soon after.) Someday, I am sure we will see each other for the first time but under better circumstances.

The last leg of my flight came around two or three o'clock in the afternoon. The weather was awesome! It was hot but with a different kind of heat. I had been shown to my sleeping quarters, and I got unpacked in no time at all. The room in the barracks was open air all the way. There were no doors or glassed-in windows. There were only shutters to close off the screen windows and in case of a rain. Evidently, there is no real cold weather on this island. Did I mention rain? Yeah, there was always plenty of rain.

The thing that bothered me the most about sleeping in an open-air facility was there was no privacy. Even the geckos made their way into the rooms twenty-four seven. Nothing like waking up in the morning with one of those little pink critters lying on your face with those big eyes staring at you! At first, it was a frightful event, but after a few nights, it became just a nuisance. Besides, the little fellows helped to keep the bug population down. There are no mosquitoes there!

Clark AFB was a huge strategic air command (SAC) base with hundreds of jets flying in and out constantly. Most of the missions were to drop bombs in Viet Nam in a moment's notice. The noise level was always loud, constant enough that eventually one did not even notice it. The barracks were a good distance from the flight line to somewhat minimize the noise level, especially at night.

This base made the Karamursel AFB in Turkey look like a boys' camp. This base was so big it took a lot of time to walk anywhere. The BX and movie theater were clear across the base from the living quarters. Where I worked was a long distance as well. Good thing we had a military bus service to help us get around. It was exhausting to go anywhere, and with the dry heat, it was impossible to get there with a dry shirt.

It did not take me long to start settling down, and eventually I had enough time to learn where everything was located on base. It is a good feeling to get your bearings and to know the layout of things. After being tied down for several weeks, I wanted to take a big step and get off base for some well-deserved R&R. I felt it would be good to see the true Philippines. There was a lot to see on the main island of Luzon. The culture was very different from that I had experienced in Turkey.

We were always cautioned never to leave base without a buddy, and it was most advisable to go off base in a group. There is a small town just outside the base named Angeles City (after Los Angeles, California.) The town was full of girls, bars, shops, and more girls. Every corner had young girls just standing around trying their best to pull in a lonesome GI in order to do "favors" and take his money. A better name for this town would have been Sin City. Better yet, Sodom or Gomorra. The US government was spending millions of dollars testing the girls in town for all sorts of diseases. The girls were "inspected" very often and wore a badge to show the last time they had seen a doctor. How sad is that? I did not like Angeles City and avoided going there for obvious reasons.

To witness the true decency of the native commoners, one would travel a few more miles outside of "Sodom." The islanders are mostly farmers. There are miles and miles of rice patties with water buffalo or caribou working in the fields. These are proud and hardworking people trying to make a decent and honorable living without sin. It is here that I learned to appreciate the true spirit of the wonderful Philippines culture.

During one of my excursions, I had purchased beautiful vases and table items made of monkey wood to ship back home. I bought a beautiful oil painting called *The Organization* from a local artist. It is a picture of Jesus and the disciples on a black velvet material. I rolled it up and hand-carried it back to America.

There is a lot of history pertaining to the island of Luzon. The Japanese had taken over the island during World War II, and eventually the Allies were able to recapture it with the help of the Filipinos. However, it was not until after thousands of soldiers had been killed in battle trying to recapture the island nation. There is a beautiful American and Philippines National Cemetery located near Tguig, Metro Manila that looks similar to the Arlington National Cemetery in Washington, DC. Known as the Manila American Cemetery and Memorial, its creation is in the memory of the 7,644 soldiers killed during WW II and buried there. It is a humble sight to see, and it reminded me as to why I had been assigned to the Philippines in the first place. Not too terribly far away though was yet another political threat to these people and to others that lived in the countries nearby. It is a shame that humans have not yet learned the lessons of war.

As usual, I stayed focused on my work. During the slow late-night shifts, I had the opportunity to learn more modern technologies than what was available in Turkey. Each day was a new adventure, as I was able to spend time in the air force library doing personal research to expand my knowledge. I was able to learn about flying saucers (UFOs), submersible objects (USOs) Mao Tse-tung, and the Viet Nam War. I guess being so close to the war zone made it more of a reality and gave cause to try to learn more and understand its purpose.

Each night after retiring to bed, the Communist guerillas living in the not so far distant mountains would shoot orange flares at each other, just to remind us they were still a threat to us all. Thus the harsh reality that anything adverse could happen at any time, and any one of those events could be life threating. In 1969, the formation of the rebellious organization known as CPP-NPA (Communist People's Party—New People's Army) and later the formation of the NDF (New Democratic Front) became so violent the president of the Philippines, Ferdinand Marcos, eventually declared martial law in 1971 (just a couple of years before I arrived). Upward of 43,000 deaths had occurred during the rebellion that eventually forced the group into the countryside where they continued their military training and operations.

Both air force military police and the Philippine Army heavily guarded the base for obvious reasons. Their primary duty was to protect the aircraft and military weapons but also to protect the intelligence-gathering mission and the military personnel and families. With the rebellious CPP-NPA just a short distance away, there was always the threat of an invasion or an attack.

I prayed constantly to God, trusting in Him to keep all us safe from harm and also that I would get a good night's sleep without fear. The nightly military action in the mountains made me feel unsafe while trying to go sleep. I always sensed something was wrong with the situation I was in, but I just could not get a solid handle on it.

One day, a friend of mine became involved in an argument with one of the local houseboys. A houseboy is usually hired to keep the barracks cleaned and could be hired to do personal laundry for a small price. I did not use the houseboys to do my laundry because I did not feel comfortable with someone else cleaning my clothes. Besides, I did not make enough money to keep myself afloat.

Presumably, the argument involved a pair of jeans stolen from my friend. The argument tragically escalated to a much graver level. The Filipinos are a proud people and take personal threats very seriously. Sadly, my friend was murdered during his sleep. His throat was slit wide open. No one saw or heard anything. It was tragic, and the incident made everyone very uncomfortable for a long time thereafter. From that day on, I kept my valuables in my pillow at night and did not show anyone what I owned. Nor did I talk to the houseboys. This incident was another reason why I did my own laundry, as I did not want any kind of altercations to occur. Mentally, the incident bothered me from then on. The incident was always on my mind. With this added fear, my prayers intensified with the additional need for protection.

The months could not go by fast enough for me. I just wanted to get back home safely to Charlene. I tried my best not to get her upset with the safety of the base and the murder on base. Nor did I talk about the constant killing of the K9 dogs used for patrolling the base. There is a huge K9 cemetery on the base due to the excessive murdering of the dogs by the Communist activists and the Filipinos. The Filipinos did not like the dogs, as they kept intruders at bay and prevented the stealing of wire and other valuables from the base that could be sold for cash.

My military orders kept changing. One day I would get orders to go to Japan, or the next month I would get orders to go to Taiwan. The next month, the orders would be for Alaska and so on and so forth. Then finally one month I received orders to go to the underground White House in Maryland. This was the one tour of duty I really wanted. I prayed to keep these orders. This assignment would have allowed Charlene to go with me once we were married. She could work on base as a civilian contractor or obtain a job off base. It was a great place to start a family as well.

My tour of duty was getting closer to the end, and then tragedy struck again. This time it was a little too close for comfort. I woke up one morning in a panic with blood oozing from my left calf. I did not know what had happened. Perhaps I got a bug bite, or I scratched it, or somehow it was seriously cut. There was a lot of blood everywhere. I cleaned up the bed and bandaged my leg to the best of my ability and then headed out toward the dispensary. My heart was pounding. What was going on? What happened? Would I be okay?

The doctor entered the waiting room and took a good look at my leg. He said it appeared that I had a cancer known as melanoma—a dangerous and deadly cancer if not treated quickly. I could not believe what I was just hearing. It was as if my life was ending. *Oh God*, I cried. *What is happening to me? Will I survive this cancer? Can it be curable? How did I get it? What caused this to happen?*

Within a flash, I was in surgery. The attending surgeon removed the tumor from the inside of my lower left calf. Easy enough, I thought. I calmed myself down, believing I would be okay and could return to life as normal. No, I was very wrong.

The surgeon said he removed a good bit of my leg tissue around the tumor, leaving a deep cut. However, it was imperative to leave immediately to return to Wilford Hall in San Antonio, Texas. The surgeon explained to me the tumor had been removed. However, the cancer could have spread throughout my body by way of the lymph glands.

My world had just turned upside down. Once again, a thousand thoughts raced throughout my head. *Will I still be able to marry Charlene? Will my career in the service end? How long will it take to find out my condition? Will I not be promoted to staff sergeant? Is there a cure for this disease? What if I do not survive this cancer? Has the devil finally won? Instead of dying in Viet Nam as a war hero, will I painfully die in a military hospital? Has death finally caught up with me?* I cried, "Oh, God, where are you? I need you!"

It did not take long to make the official arrangements to catch the next military flight back to the States. I packed my gear, said my good-byes to everyone, and sent a telegram back home to the family:

> [Stop] Going to Wilford Hall Hospital San Antonio
> [Stop] I have cancer [Stop] Will call you when I can
> [Stop] I love you all [Stop]

It was one of the most tragic and miserable days in my life. Was I being punished for complaining about guard duty at San Angelo? Was I being punished for all of the wrongdoing that I had committed while growing up? Was this it? Everyone cautioned me not to sign up for the service; go to Canada instead! Go to college or else you will wind up dead in Viet Nam. *Well, is this my "Viet Nam?" Did I get into some Agent Orange? Were there deadly chemicals fired up in the mountains at night that somehow entered into my body?*

That evening I sat quietly at the base headquarters while my papers were drafted to order me back to stateside. It was like a death sentence. It quickly became a thousand-mile march toward the end of my life. Depression set in quickly, and I did not want to talk to anyone about anything. *Just get me out of this place!* I was not the same person anymore. I had lost my will to live, and nothing meant anything to me. Nothing! I felt abandoned by my God. I did not want to talk to Him. Once again, I was a nuisance and was not needed or wanted by anyone, perhaps not even God. In self-pity, I was snickering to myself, *Who is touching me now?*

> Let us therefore come boldly unto the throne of grace, that we may obtain mercy, and find grace to help in time of need.
> —Hebrews 4:16 (KJV)

The Testing of Faith
Ω

I felt as though someone had placed me in a glass jar. I could hear my own breathing and nothing else. People stared at me. Occasionally I would return a glazed-eye look without a response. It was as if they knew something was wrong about me, but I did not care. "He is coming from overseas," they would say. "He is not all there," others would surmise. "Perhaps he got into drugs in Nam," some would speculate. "No, he is just war torn," others would say.

The military flight back to Guam was a lonely and cold experience. I sat in the back of a cold military plane in a net, similar to the contraption used to hold down cargo. The noise level of the roaring engines was deafening. We flew into Guam just long enough to drop the back-end door of the plane down to pick up a few other GIs. They were intensely running, almost as one. It was raining heavily, and a major storm was taking its toll on the island. No sooner than the back end of the plane touched the ground, it was off again and rising swiftly into the air. Just long enough for the drenched GIs to run quickly on board. They were running with all of their might and practically falling into the cargo plane just to hold on.

As the cargo door closed, I noticed a huge, soaking wet, black American soldier as big as two men, with no boots. He quietly lay down next to me in the net seating. I could see the deep darkness in his eyes. With his pant legs rolled up, it was obvious he was loosely bound at the feet with a heavy chain. With each striking lightning bolt, I could see his naked but immaculate torso reflecting the strength of a mighty man. His feet were soiled, and I could not help but notice his duck-like webbed toes. In a deep sense, I felt just like him—bound by chains with no hope of getting free. He did not say a word as the rainwater poured off his strong but fragile frame. No one bothered to give him a towel or offer comfort of any kind. I felt so sorry for him and wept silently as the thunder pounded all around us.

There was a deep silence beneath the roaring noise of the plane as the darkness and the night found us sleeping for what seemed to be an eternity—just like the lengthy night of riding in the back of a car from my childhood dreams. Only this time the casual light was from the lightning shining into the small windows of the plane. It allowed me to see a glimpse of everyone aboard the cargo plane during this long trip home.

I do not remember stopping anywhere along the way. Not even a midstop in Hawaii, just perhaps a straight flight. If there was a stop, I slept through it. Before I knew it, the plane was landing at Travis AFB, not too far from Oakland, California. How appropriate. It seemed like an omen that we had flown to Travis AFB. (I discovered many years later that I was born in Vallejo, not far away. It is where I had my beginning in life.) We must have flown all night and into the next day. It was hours after landing when I finally settled into one of the barracks on base for a long sleep. I really did not care if anything should happen to me while I slept. I did not care even to wake up. Just let me die and get it all over. It did not matter one way or the other to me. My life was over as far as I was concerned. I was exhausted. I was so depressed, and all I wanted to do was sleep. I felt my faith in God had slipped away. I went to sleep knowing I was inching toward the end of my life.

The next evening, I found my way to the mess hall to get something to eat. My next flight would be within a few days, thus giving me the time to try to get my thoughts and reasoning straight. I had to catch a military flight to Arizona and then to Kelly AFB in San Antonio. Then I would catch a military bus to Wilford Hall. Nothing really mattered or was urgent at the time. Just eat, sleep, and wonder what would happen next. As a result of my transfer into medical status, my expected promotion was on an indefinite hold. Go figure. My dream job was lost. My expected life with Charlene was just a dream, I guessed. Would she have anything to do with me once I told her about my illness? I had an empty feeling, and I was scared. I was a lost cause and a pitiful example of an elite soldier.

Then one day while walking around the barracks, I came across an old and forgotten face. Jay, of all the people in this world, was at the same barracks! I had given up on him a long time ago. He had gone AWOL again, and this time he was on his way back home. He had received a dishonorable discharge. I could tell his brain was fried from drugs, and this once good school friend was no longer able to carry a decent conversation. I guess my situation was not as bad as Jay's. Deep down inside as I hoped for a chance to live, this good friend had already died inside. To this day, I do not know what became of him. I have not seen him at any of our high school reunions. It is almost as if he disappeared off the face of the earth. I was never able to locate his family. I had hoped he would be okay and perhaps someday we might see each other but in a better state of mind. I guess seeing this old friend again helped me to focus on something other than my own sorry situation. At least for a few days anyway. Did God purposely send me back to Travis to try to help Jay? If He did, then I failed to do His will. I felt so sorry I could not have helped Jay at the time. I was simply in no mental condition to help myself.

Unintentionally, I had lost track of the months, weeks, and days I had remaining while in the Philippines, and day zero did not seem so important anymore. The thrill of coming home again did not even register a moment of happiness. The joy just was not there to make any difference. There was no need now to count the months, weeks, or days. I was on a new countdown. The countdown to the possible end of my life here on earth. At the moment, I really did not care.

A few days later, I arrived at Wilford Hall Air Force Medical Center in San Antonio, Texas. Soon after checking into the hospital, I was assigned to a bed up on the third or fourth floor. This was a dormitory-like floor with row after row of beds. Once again no privacy. After a quick scanning of the room, I realized its occupants were all terminally ill patients. Was this God's way of telling me to get my act together? Was it necessary to put me on this floor? Was this an out-of-the-box wakeup call? Not only was I staring death in the face with my own life, but I was seeing it firsthand. Death was lingering over the many beds filled with terminally ill patients from all parts of the world. Military men and women just like me. I cried and cried for them. I could feel and see their pain and suffering.

Lying in the bed next to me was a man with a belly the size of a washtub. He had a very rare disease that caused his stomach to bloat to this massive size. He always had a smile on his face, and I always wondered if any of the doctors could help him. Eventually, he died one night from his stomach rupturing. I felt so lost and sorry for his family. The medical staff drew flimsy curtains around my bed as they prepared his body for the morgue situated in the basement. *Dear God, be with him and his family. If I should die soon, my Lord, just let me die in my sleep.* This was definitely a wakeup call, and I could not sleep for nights after the incident. I knew now firsthand that God was trying to get my attention. His message was clear—not to be so self-centered and to realize there are others in this world that are a lot worse than I am. Where was my faith? I was ashamed of myself. How could I turn against my Lord and best friend?

I finally had the chance to call home and to tell Dad and Mom Grant the situation. They made plans to drive to San Antonio to see me. I wanted them to speak with the doctors and to help me understand what the consequences would be. Eventually I was assigned to a lieutenant colonel who specialized in plastic surgery. He was straightforward and harsh in many ways. After getting to know him better, I nicknamed him Dr. Super. He seemed to have my interest at hand and was ready to get on with the various tests and labs. My parents were very pleased to meet with him and felt confident in his approach. What, if anything, could he do for me? Only time would tell.

It was February 1974 when I first entered the hospital. Several months had gone by, and it seemed that I had every test and lab imaginable. I was tired of being prodded, poked, and infused day in and day out. I never dreamed that anyone could dream up the equipment, medicines, and tests that I was being subjected to on a daily basis. Every early morning and every late-ending day was filled with a multitude of tests. I soon learned how efficient and dedicated the medical staff remained during my long stay. God gave me a blessing when He sent me to these good people at Wilford Hall. I can never repay them for the care they gave me during this difficult time in my life.

Concerned, Mom Grant said I had run up the family telephone bill to over $300 a month. Every call was nothing but a distant conversation filled with fearful tears. She begged me to stop calling and to try getting a grip on things. I did not know I was even making those calls. Amazing how the mind plays tricks on a person when subjected to such drastic conditions. Mom Grant contacted Dr. Super and advised him of the situation. There was nothing he could do other than to slow down on the tests and try to find something for me to do. As a result, I became the resident patient pusher that wheeled patients to their tests and lab work. The telephone bills dropped as I began to feel a sense of worth and needed for something other than as a guinea pig.

One day in April, after several months of wondering when all of the testing would stop, I finally got up the nerve to start voicing my anger as to when the tests would stop. Something needed to be finalized! I needed more communication as to what action the doctors and staff were taking toward my healing.

When the surgeons removed the whole tumor at Clark AFB, they sent it to a tumor registry. Somehow, it was lost. Without the pathological test results, there was no way of knowing if 100 percent of the tumor had been removed. If the tumor and associated medical records could not be located, then I was facing an amputation of my left leg. Not a very pretty picture for a twenty-year-old kid. In addition, my chances of survival past the age of twenty-five would be less than 35 percent if no amputation took place. Only the surgical procedure would determine the true percentages. It really depended on how far the cancer had spread and at what stage it had entered. Stage 4 meant no hope of survival for any length of time. My heart sank deeper. How much more bad news could I take?

It was a hard decision to make. *Do I accept my fate for what it is? On the other hand, do I agree to have my leg removed?* Did the professionals really know how far the cancer had spread? Why couldn't the tumor be found? Where was it?

My parents were upset with the idea of having my leg removed. Dad Grant had contacted Congressman Jim Wright. He explained to him how important it was for the medical records to be located immediately. It was a matter of my losing a leg and having a normal life or having a reduced life. Could the congressman help to save my leg? Surely, he could do something to find those records!

It was May by now, and the day of the surgery finally arrived. I would wake up without a leg, and I would know then how far the cancer had spread. No matter what, my life as a whole being was getting closer to a probable end, and whatever God had planned for me was definitely in His hands. I prayed for the first time in a long time. I just had not felt like praying because of my anger toward Him. Now I realized I was not in control of my life. I had to accept there were other men and women on that ward who were in worse shape than I was. They needed to be healed more than I did. So if God needed to give them more help than me, then I understood. He had already helped to save me once in Turkey, and asking for a second chance at survival did not seem fair to the others. (The Bible supports that such a prayer offered in sincere faith will heal the sick, and the Lord will make one well.)

It was nearly an all-day surgical event. The medical team stripped out my lymph nodes and the main artery from my left groin all the way down my left leg. Samples of these were sent to the pathologist for testing, and the results came back showing clear of any minute cancer cells. However, it was too late. Then reconstructive work began, and muscle and skin were removed from my right thigh to cover the knee once the left leg was amputated.

A few weeks before the surgery, I endured a Lymphangiogram test. To conduct this test, the patient is to lay flat on his/her back. Then a blue contrast dye is injected into a small slit made across the top of the patient's feet. Once administered, the dye can be seen by the naked eye as it travels throughout the legs and up into the torso area. Once the dye enters the lungs, it dissipates. The dye had performed well while moving up my right leg; however, it never went past my left knee.

This test led to the decision to amputate my left leg. The thinking was that the cancer had spread in my left leg lymph nodes and thus perhaps throughout my body. The doctors were hoping the cancer had not gone past the knee, so amputation would stop it in its tracks.

It was several days before I was able to comprehend what had just happened a few days before. I had been on my back and given morphine for pain. The surgery was a traumatic shock to my body.

Fortunately, I was in very good shape physically due to my training. If I had been that previous ninety-pound weakling fresh out of school, I might not have survived the surgery or endured the pain. God's timing was perfect.

The pain medications kept me heavily sedated after the surgery, so I slept the following few days. Eventually, I woke up, and to my surprise, Charlene and her mother were sitting next to my bed. It was as if I had awakened from a long dream. At first I thought I was dreaming or even dead. Oh, I was far from being dead—a little weird from the drugs but not dead. Charlene was so beautiful ... just as I remembered the night of our first date. Her beautiful hair was hanging so elegantly around her shining face. She touched me on my shoulder and asked how I was feeling. I really did not know for sure, but I knew having her at my side was a blessing.

Her mother had driven them down for the weekend to see me. They had been at the hospital just a day or so when I finally came around. I felt a little embarrassed of course. My naked presence was not the best of circumstances to be seeing a hopeful future mother-in-law.

Then it hit me. Should I dare look to see if my leg was gone? I had a huge tent-like structure hovering over my body, and I felt a lot of warmth under the contraption. What was this all about? I finally glanced under the tent-like dome and then realized something went terribly wrong. I still had my leg, but it was all cut up from my left abdomen side down to my left foot. I was stark naked, and there must have been at least a hundred stitches and staples all up and down my leg. Where the tumor used to be was a huge indention the size of a football going around my left calf. I could tell my calf had been removed down to the bone. Surprisingly there were two pieces of new baby-like skin covering the area stitched together. I noticed a bulky heat lamp under my "tent" to keep me warm and to provide drying of the many excreting fluids.

Nevertheless, why was my right thigh hurting? I glanced at it. Evidently, the baby-like layer of skin on my left leg was surgically removed from my upper right thigh. Was I ever in a mess! It was evident that this would take several months to heal. *Lord God, what has happened? Was I cured of the cancer? Why didn't the amputation happen? Where is Dr. Super?*

When the pathologist reported the now removed lymph nodes were all clear of cancer cells, it raised a red flag and immediately the team of specialists changed their game plan. They decided to investigate the area where the tumor once had been. It was then they found the reason why the dye did not move upward. Evidently, the surgeon in the Philippines had dug deep enough into my leg (really close to the bone) that he managed to get out all of the tumor and its feelers! However, what about the dye test? Well, the dye could not move upward because of the excessive scar tissue remaining in the surgical area.

I was one lucky man. The amputation had been called off, and only a large area of my left calf was removed. The replacement tissue came from a donor sight from my right upper thigh. Then a hundred stitches to patch things up. Dr. Super told me a few days later I had proved the Lymphangiogram test to be inconclusive. He assured me this test would never be used by the military as a basis for final decision making on such matters. God had given me my leg back, and He gave me a second chance to keep my life! What a miracle!

My heart sank, as I did not know how long this would take to heal, and knowing how ugly this looked, our wedding plans would be on hold for a long time and maybe called off all together. I doubted that Charlene would want to continue being engaged to a cripple. I was so embarrassed after realizing my nakedness and did not want Charlene and her mom to notice my condition. I was not for certain they knew how bad I looked and hoped they did not care as long as I was going to be okay. What was going through Charlene's mind at this time? Was her mom being supportive? Would there be reservations about our future together?

Charlene and her mom had to leave, but Charlene promised to come back soon. Mom and Dad Grant had come down with my younger brother Sid. It was great to see them again. Especially seeing Sid again made my whole day. I was beginning to feel better and soon became uncomfortable and agitated just lying in bed all day and night. After a few days, bedsores started to appear, so the nursing staff would turn me several times a day. I was not able to move on my own. It was so embarrassing.

Every day was just another struggle to be still so as not to tear open any stitches or cause additional bleeding. The heat lamps seemed to be getting hotter and hotter, and I just wanted to get up and move around if just for a moment. Just to cool down and to stretch my body would have been a great relief.

Finally, after a couple of more weeks of madness, Dr. Super told me I could sit up and dangle my feet on the side of the bed. Oh, the joy of being able to dangle my feet! He cautioned we would have to take many baby steps. Due to the severity of my surgery, I would have to learn how to walk again. Can you imagine being twenty years old and not knowing how to walk? It was not long before I could stand up with the help of my nurse aides. It was then I realized Dr. Super was right about learning how to walk again. Just standing next to the bed was a major ordeal, and two minutes was like a lifetime of agonizing pain and struggling to balance. *Will I ever walk again? Will I have to use crutches or a wheelchair from now on?*

My God is a loving God, and He had not forgotten me. He made it happen for me to be strong enough to stand up and walk again. God brought back Lazarus from the dead, so I knew He had no problem helping me to walk again. I could just hear Him say, "Stand and be tall. Surely your faith is strong enough to heal your wounds.

Walk, my son, walk." A few weeks later, I was walking with caution and with a lot of straining to the door of my room and back to the bed. In the book of John 5:8, Jesus tells an invalid, "Rise, take up thy bed, and walk" (KJV). I can testify to this day that the ability to get up and walk again is truly a wonderful feeling to experience.

To my joyous surprise, Charlene came to visit me again. She was on vacation and decided to spend some time with me. What a blessing! There was no joy ever so good than to have her coming to my bedside every day, all day. Finally, with her at my side, I was strong enough to walk back and forth from my bed and then to the door and back without too much pain or weakness. Charlene kept me in good company, and we were able to rekindle our love for each other. How amazing it was to confirm she still loved me and wanted to be with me even though I was more or less crippled. Her devotion and love for me were greater than I had first imagined.

Eventually, I was able to walk with Charlene out the door and to the nurses' station across the way and then back. Each week I was making a little better progress than the week before. My stitches were holding up fairly well. The watered-down blood oozing from my grafts and donor sight was finally slowing down. The heat lamps were doing the trick of drying the wounds, and I was beginning to feel human again. Then came the big surprise! It was time to remove the stitches and staples from my body. Charlene was able to assist. I have never seen so many staples and stitches! I looked like a walking corpse just after an autopsy! After what seemed to be an eternity of plucking, it was finally over. A few hours of pain and agony gave me the confirmation that I was getting better. In addition, a real shower to boot!

Charlene and I had talked about getting married in late June, but that did not happen. We had to postpone the wedding to late July, as Dr. Super just did not think I had enough strength in my left leg to walk for any length of time. A few more weeks, and I gained the much-needed momentum to be strong enough to walk outside of my room with crutches and down to the end of the hallway and back to my bed. I was not getting out of breath, and the oozing of blood from the left calf had stopped. However, I still had some bleeding issues with my upper right thigh at the donor sight.

On July 20, 1974, our wedding day became a reality! My faith was stronger than ever, and I did not want to miss my wedding day again. Dr. Super finally gave me permission to go home as long as I returned the following Sunday. What a bummer. At least I was going to be stepping out of that hospital for three days and would get to see my family and friends again. It had been over five long months since my admittance into the hospital. However, it seemed like an eternity.

When I first arrived in the Philippines, I started the process of getting Charlene and her family cleared by the OSI so we could get married. The OSI policy is to perform an extensive background check on any existing or new relative who would be in close contact with a military intelligence agent. Since I had obtained a top-secret clearance, the OSI wanted to make certain my future in laws and spouse had a background check to prevent me from getting into a potential harmful relationship. It was a matter of national security as well. Having a top-secret clearance has its privileges, but it also has some drawbacks. Charlene and her family had to be officially cleared by the OSI, or I simply could not marry her and remain in my official capacity. I knew wholeheartedly they would not have any problems since her father worked for a major aircraft-manufacturing firm. After the documents were filed, Charlene and her family received their clearance within just a few weeks. Praise God! I would have made the decision to leave the service had they not cleared. I was okay with that! Nothing was going to keep us from getting married! So I thought at the time.

Charlene's cousin, Jessie, stood up as her bridesmaid, and Jessie's husband became my groomsman. We selected a small Catholic church in Irving and picked a Saturday evening for the wedding. It was the best of all days! I think my nerves were at the level of breaking apart that day. I was afraid of Charlene not marrying me and running away, and even worse, I was terrified knowing she could divorce me if things did not go well. I just wanted us to be happy, healthy, and financially okay. Well, one out of three is not so bad. Being happy together is most important, and it simply makes a marriage the best, especially when God is at the center of the family.

The wedding turned out to be awesome even though I knelt down during the whole ceremony. Charlene followed my lead so that I would not be embarrassed. We had a simple wedding reception afterward at the church, and then it was off to the hotel. We stayed at the Green Oaks Inn located in far west Fort Worth. I had booked the same room where Elvis Presley stayed. Charlene wanted to marry Elvis, but he was not available at the time. We are both big fans!

After we arrived at the hotel, we began unloading the car. While standing on the second-floor balcony, Charlene managed to dump rice all over me while I was unloading the luggage below. I did not see that coming! Then I managed to break a bottle of champagne and got the bubbly all over the place. Little did I know the rest of our marriage would be one big continuous laugh and disaster after another! We both slept fairly well that night, as we were simply exhausted. The next day, we went to church and visited my Grandmother and Grandad Johnson.

I hated to leave my new bride, but the time came down to the line. I had to get back to San Antonio as promised. If I did not return, I would have been considered AWOL. No jail time for this guy! Besides, I would not be able to handle living in a jail cell with the need for medical attention and with a new bride by herself. It was definitely a great weekend but a sad one. I simply did not want to leave Charlene. I knew she would be safe living with her folks until I was able to get out of the hospital. It was near the end of July, and it was going to be a lonesome and hard few months ahead. I really missed Charlene and wanted nothing more than to return home.

"God, be at my side always and give me my strength and hope. Strengthen my faith so I may keep thy commandments and do thy will. Bless my new wife and me forever more and help us to grow with you for years to come! You are my salvation, my redeemer! You have given me my legs and taught me to walk. Now I shall walk for you to do your will and to sing your praises. For you are my God and my heavenly Father for whom I shall be forever a faithful servant."

> Now faith is the substance of things hoped for, the evidence of things not seen.
> —Hebrews 11:1 (KJV)

The Loss of a Brother
Ω

Within a few years after arriving to the boys' school in Arkansas, Noel had to leave because of their age restrictions. About the age of fifteen, in 1971, he had been admitted to the Lena Pope foster home in Fort Worth. The person in charge of his care was a very bad influence, for her own selfish reasons, and this upset Dad Grant very much. Mom Grant became so afraid of Noel she would not allow him to call us or visit us. It was determined many months later he was missing a chromosome, thus the reason for his swaying moods and issues. A subscription of tranquilizers several months prior to leaving for Arkansas was prescribed in an attempt to calm him down and to smooth out his mood swings. They helped some, but they kept him too sedated and acting much like a zombie. While taking this medicine, we noticed Noel was not the same person as during his younger years. His personality had totally changed, leaving him sometimes lifeless. It became evident to me he was no longer the same brother I had grown up with.

My childhood brother Noel loved all animals and could tell you the name of birds with accuracy. In 1975, at the age of eighteen, he trained birds and animals for the Casa Manana in Fort Worth. He was in the process of training a falcon for the well-known production *Swift Family Robinson* on the day he died. The bird had flown to the top of a telephone pole during a training session and would not come down upon Noel's commands. In aggravation, he climbed the pole, retrieved the bird, and fell do his death into an electric transformer.

With much sorrow in my heart, it had been at least six years since I had seen Noel last, and news of his death hit me hard. Dad Grant, Sid, and I attended the funeral without Mom Grant. It was a very hard funeral to attend, and I know Dad Grant felt he was the cause of Noel's demise, as he felt guilty for sending him to the Lena Pope home. I think Mom Grant felt even worse, as it was her fear of Noel's actions that kept him at bay. He always had that special Irish boy look about him, but due to his severe burning from the electricity, we were not able to view him at the service. Out of respect for the family, the casket was not opened for viewing of the body.

Charlene and I had been married a year in July 1975, and she had never seen Noel. In a very unusual but miraculous way, we both would get to see Noel down the road many years later. God had a plan that would soon heal my longing to see him just one more time.

It is written in 1 Samuel 18 that the "Soul of Jonathan" was knit with the "Soul of David." Jonathan loved him as his own soul. Then Jonathan and David made a covenant with each other. Noel and I had such a commitment that we became like blood brothers, protecting and supporting the other when in need. We had even cut our fingers one day and exchanged blood to confirm our blood-brother bonding. It was a great moment!

The Bible tells us in Proverbs 18:24 that Jesus "is a friend that sticketh closer than a brother" (KJV). It is such a tragic thing to lose loved ones; seeing them depart from our lives—well, for some, it is just too much to bear. Thankfully, our Lord is eternally gracious and will in turn make a way for us and our dearly departed to be bonded together forever as family once again for eternity. Jesus is family. He loved his earthly family, Joseph and Mary, very much, just as He loves us.

John 11 tells us the heartfelt story concerning the death of Lazarus, whom Jesus loved and raised from the dead. He loved Mary, Martha, and Lazarus very much; they were his extended family, just as we sometimes have our extended families! After watching them weep over their brother's death, Jesus too wept (John 11:35). Jesus knows when we are hurting over the departure of our loved ones, and we should be in comfort knowing He too is weeping with us.

I will never forget the special childhood years that Noel and I had together. I visit his grave often just to reminisce about our times together and to dream about what our lives could have been together. I am certain he would have been a great veterinarian or a famous animal trainer in his own right. Even today while writing this book, it is hard to hold back the tears as I think about what could have been.

> To everything there is a season, and a time to every purpose under the heaven: A time to be born, and a time to die; a time to embrace, and time to refrain from embracing.
> —Ecclesiastes 3:1, 2, 5b (KJV)

The Court-Martial

Ω

Soon the day of my provisional dismissal from the service came, and I was able to leave Wilford Hall. There was an empty place nurturing within my heart. I was going to miss all of the orderlies, the many nurses, numerous doctors, and many friends that I had become acquainted with. Unbelievably, I was going to miss the room where I had lived for a good part of my twentieth year. All of the events that took place over the last several months were now a part of my past. It was almost a dream now. The daily tests, the needles, the food, the pain and suffering, and the many tears that families and friends shed. I am not certain how medical personnel get over such emotions and daily trauma. It is something that still bothers me even today. I cowardly faint during blood tests and get a sickening feeling when I go to a hospital for treatment, tests, or just to visit a friend. Like a baby, I still cry when pricked for blood or when I go to the hospital to see the sick, and I remember those who died next to me and those who have suffered more than I have.

My daily prayer to God each morning is for Him to cure those who are sick and suffering. It is a terrible thing for anyone to have to suffer from diseases or deformities or to be stuck in a hospital for any reason. If God should not have it in His will to heal these of need, then I pray the pain of those suffering to be subdued, for suffering with pain in spite of an illness is an undo punishment that should not have to be endured.

After my release from the hospital in October 1974, I was placed on temporary military duty. I was assigned to live at my home in order to continue recovering and regaining my strength. I was officially required to return to the hospital every two weeks for follow-up treatments and testing. I am thankful to have this benefit because of the medical complications I was enduring. The constant swelling of my left leg was becoming a big issue. Should it not go down, then gangrene would set in, and eventually I would lose my leg. The doctors gave me a few years before this would become a possible reality. It was a medical probability the leg would most likely need to be amputated around the age of thirty-five. Not a comforting thought.

It was a blessing that I went to work for Dad Grant as a bookkeeper and was able to keep my leg propped up on a box during the day. I was continuously having problems with my right thigh not healing as well. It would take over a year for this donor sight to stop bleeding and to get back to normal. I would use large gauzes to cover the area and replace them several times a day. The touching of the fabric from my pants would keep the area irritated and constantly bleeding.

Religiously, I would drive back to the hospital every two weeks as directed for treatments and testing, always being conscientious of my assignment to do exactly as instructed and to report in a timely manner to my doctors. I had this unusual fear of being reprimanded for not following orders. I was still enlisted in the military and was obligated to follow the rules no matter what excuse prevailed. Upon each arrival, I would sign in and report to Dr. Super's staff. When the tests were completed and Dr. Super was satisfied, I would head back home until the next scheduled appointment.

In October 1974, the unforeseeable and shocking news arrived in my mailbox. I received a certified registered letter from the Staff Judge Advocates Office at Lackland AFB. It was a notice to appear in court, in dress uniform, on a certain date and time. Failure to appear as ordered would result in my immediate arrest. The court had assigned a military attorney to my case, so there was no need for other counsel. According to the documents, if found guilty, I was going to be court-martialed! Court-martialed! For what?

It was such a shocking and frightening experience. There were no words to describe the roller coaster of feelings and emotions going through my head. I was totally at a loss for words. What could I have possibly done? I had an excellent military record—or so I thought. Not to mention the honors received for my achievements. I always followed my orders to the T. Why was I being court-martialed?

Had I not been through enough misery and suffering already? I would have thought the past several months of agony and suffering while confined in the hospital as proof I could not have done anything wrong or outside the law. "Lord, what is going on? Have You forsaken me? What should I do?"

Charlene and I were in a state of panic and practically in tears. I called Dr. Super and explained to him what I had just received in the mail. He could not believe what he was hearing as I read the letter to him. As a lieutenant colonel, Dr. Super had been my superior officer for the past several months. He was appalled at what the government was trying to pursue. He told me to report early the Monday morning of the hearing, and he would be there to support me 100 percent.

I met with the court-ordered assigned attorney as anticipated the morning of the hearing. He was a bright young major. His first question was to ask what had I done to deserve the court-martial. I explained to him how long I had been in the hospital and gave a brief nonclassified version of my prior military experiences. It was our understanding the government was accusing me of deliberately staging my illness in order to get out of the service. They insisted I knew about the tumor on my left leg when I joined the service and did not disclose the situation during my initial Dallas physical—none of which was true. How could I have known a cancer tumor was in my body? I did not even know about such things. Absurd!

He told me about the courtroom setup and how to expect it so as not to be frightened. Just like in the movies, it would be a large, somewhat dark room with a single chair in the middle. In addition, a semicircle of chairs would be at one end of the room. He said I would get questions left and right but to answer only yes or no. If I had a doubt, I was to watch his reactions. In the event I did have to go into any kind of detailed answer, he warned me to be honest and tell the truth.

The evening passed quickly, and it finally came time for the big hearing. Just as promised, Dr. Super showed up to assist and to give his support. Initially, the three of us were called into the "torture chamber." I was instructed to sit in the chair that sat in the middle of the huge, somewhat darkened room. I could feel my heart beating ninety to nothing. I was so nervous I could hear my teeth chattering. The sweat began to roll down my legs, and for a moment, I did not even notice the pain in my left leg.

Just as expected, there were numerous top brass and legal experts sitting in a semicircle of chairs behind a very white and heavily starched cotton-clothed table. They appeared to be giants with very crude looks upon their faces. I have never seen so many high-ranking officers assembled in one room in all of my life! This reminded me of the news briefs that Congress would have when interrogating civilians, suspecting crooks, and diplomats. Now me. I was a proposed criminal. How could I begin to tell anyone as to how embarrassing and awful this situation made me feel? Especially after all of the trauma and pain I suffered over the last several months and was still enduring!

The highly decorated person in the middle must have been the staff judge advocate general who spoke softly and asked me to remain seated. I felt like a criminal as the light shined brightly upon my body. Every ray of light penetrated deep within my figure, such that not even a shadow would be cast on the floor. Sweat poured down my underarms, and my legs were quivering enough to make a noise that even the walls could hear. *God, what have I done so wrong to deserve this kind of torture!* I just wanted to cry. I guess the uniform I was wearing gave me enough strength and stamina not to crack a tear and honorably keep my composure. A vision of my military training on what to do if ever caught by the enemy slowly flashed across my mind. I never dreamed that training would be so helpful. Come on, folks. I am a good person. I am on your side!

Then, the man in the middle asked, "How are you doing?" My voice box could hardly reply, "Okay, I guess." He noticed I was very nervous, and a few chuckles came from the table. Then the interrogators from left to right began to question me. To my surprise, they wanted to know personal stuff. Stuff like was I working, and if so, what kind of work and where I was staying? They wanted to confirm if my everyday life was normal or affected by my condition. I was somewhat relieved the questioning was so personal, and despite as previously directed, I could not just answer a simple yes or no. Naturally, they asked what work I had performed for the air force, and obviously I replied it was not something I could discuss. (Most likely, this was a trick question.)

Eventually, after a few other insignificant questions, I was directed to sit down outside the courtroom. Finally, I felt more relaxed and was able to go outside the torture chamber to regain my composure. I went to the men's restroom to try drying off from the unwanted sweat. The temperature in the waiting area was drastically cooler, so my blood pressure began to drop immediately, and I began to feel more normal but chilled.

It was now my attorney and Dr. Super left behind in the courtroom, addressing the group and answering their additional questions. After about an hour, they came out, and I noticed a sigh of relief on their faces. I was so relieved, as now I felt confident I was not going to jail. Then it hit me—perhaps there was something more they needed to tell me about the matter.

Dr. Super said I would be okay and to keep in touch. He apologized for having to leave abruptly, as he needed to get to the hospital. We shook hands, and I thanked him for coming. I felt as though a lifelong friend suddenly vanished from my life as he scurried out of the building.

My attorney asked me to return to his office, as he had additional information to share and needed some documents signed. I wanted just one question put to rest. "Am I going to jail, sir?" He replied, "Not on my shift, son." I felt as though a one-ton weight had just been lifted off my shoulders, and my sense of dignity had been gracefully restored.

I immediately returned to the attorney's office where he informed me of the hearing results and praised I had done well. He said the court found no fault of my own and agreed the government should have never sent me to a tropical assignment, as this just aggravated my situation without my knowledge. The government knew during my initial physical back in Dallas that I had a possible melanoma tumor on my left calf and did not address the issue at that time. It was about recruitment numbers counting the most during the Viet Nam War, and the military needed me to help fill their required quota. Regardless of most conditions, young men were being hurried through the cattle stalls in the Dallas recruiting and physical building like there was no tomorrow.

The government dropped all of their charges and agreed to give me disability pay and medical coverage due to their "oversight." I am very thankful, as I have spent many years dealing with this disability, and medical issues have continued to haunt me over the years. As a young adolescent, I did not realize the severity of my condition. Nor did I understand how much medical attention I would need going forward. God has a loving way of taking care of fools like me. In a roundabout manner, this has been a blessing. The court dismissed all of their charges against me because the full-scaled body photos taken at my induction proved the attending doctors knew about the tumor. They obviously failed to mention it to anyone. In addition, they knew not to allow my assignments to include a tropical climate, as this would aggravate the tumor, thus causing bodily harm.

Eventually, after months of continued medical treatment, I was able to raise enough money to buy an extremity pump for $3,000 that would provide compressed air against my leg. At the time, military insurance would not cover the product. I wear a customized "boot" that covers my entire left leg up to my groin on most nights. This boot connects to the compression pump and gently compresses airtight against my leg to force the fluids into my groin area. Once the fluids flow into the abdomen, the body moves the fluids to the kidneys, and then they are extracted through the urine. It is a cumbersome process that keeps me awake at night, but after all of the years of dealing with this repeatedly, I am more or less accustomed to it.

I have found the change in weather will cause increased swelling, and if I sit too long, walk, or run too much, the swelling increases. Without the lymph nodes in my left groin and left leg, my body has to rely on the contraction of the muscles and the compression pump to remove the excessive fluids. The lymph nodes in the body are much like an oil filter on a car. My greatest fear is getting gangrene, bacteria, or injury to my left leg. Any one of these can be cause for a trip to the hospital for antibiotics or special medical treatments.

A few years after the great court-martial hearing, I received sad news. My dear friend Dr. Super decided to retire and moved to San Diego, California. I did get a call from him and was thankful he would see me at any time if needed. This "super" man was devoted to saving my leg. I will always be indebted to him for this kindness. God touched Dr. Super and gave him the knowledge and direction to help a young soldier to regain as near a perfect life as possible for years to come.

I thank God for His divine intervention of saving my leg and for getting me "clean" with the government. This court case was His way of obtaining the much-needed medical attention that I so desperately needed to go forward with my life. Once again, He has blessed me.

> Fear thou not; for I[am] with thee: be not dismayed; for I[am] thy God: I will strengthen thee; yea I will help thee; yea, I will uphold thee with the right hand of my righteousness.
> —Isaiah 41:10 (KJV)

It's Absolutely Beautiful!

Ω

My grandma Johnson and I were the best of friends. She taught me how to dance, how to sew, how to draw and paint. She taught me right from wrong, how to sing, how to make potholders, and so much more. She was a true believer in God. It was during my first year in high school that Grandmother suffered from breast cancer and had a double mastectomy. Then in September 1986, a sudden tragedy caught the family off guard when Grandad Johnson passed away. Soon after his burial, Grandmother received a shocking diagnosis of pancreatic cancer. Mom Grant had moved her to the Haltom Retirement Center not far from our home in order to have her closer to us. I hated she had to leave her home, as I just knew she would not be able to return. Grandmother's house remained locked up, empty, and lifeless for a long time afterward. Sadly, the house never seemed alive anymore. It was as though it too was enduring a slow, undesirable death. I would go by there every now and then and would reminisce about the good times.

Mom Grant went to see Grandmother daily, promptly arriving around eight in the morning in order to see the doctors. One morning in February 1987, she arrived as usual and cheerfully entered Grandmother's room. Laying down her purse, she told Grandmother she was going down the hall to get some coffee. When Mom Grant returned, Grandmother was surprisingly sitting on the edge of the bed. Grandmother was looking up at the ceiling of the room; she had her hands lifted in the air as to be in a praising fashion. She said, "Virginia (Mom Grant's first name), it is absolutely beautiful! It is absolutely beautiful!" Then ever so gently, she lay back down in her hospital bed, just as before, and solemnly passed away.

I will never forget this wonderful love of my life. Grandmother always treated me like a true grandson and loved Noel and Sid just as much. She meant the world to us, and we will never forget our blessed experiences together. Even though we tested her patience, she always took the time to tell us about God and to share with us her love of gospel music and the Bible. If I remember correctly, Jimmy Swaggart was her favorite musical artist; however, she loved the song "My Cup Runneth over with Love" by Ed Ames. As true to her life, her cup was always running over with her love for everyone. Surely God will always surround our grandma and grandpa Johnson.

If anything, I learned from my grandparents that God uses these kinds of relationships to develop our character and to strengthen our faith. We should take each day at a time to love those around us, to learn from those relationships, and to develop our faith to endure life's unexpected events.

> When I call to remembrance the unfeigned faith that is in thee, which dwelt first in thy grandmother ... and thy mother ... and I am persuaded that in thee also.
> —2 Timothy 1:5 (KJV)

Plenty of Sunshine
Ω

Charlene took good care of me and helped me to continue to heal. Without her beside me, I do not think I would have been able to get back on the right path to better health, and certainly I would not have become closer to our Lord. I continued to go back and forth to San Antonio for checkups and to report my condition to the Tumor Registry Board. I never was certain as to what this reporting was all about, but every six months, it was a routine ritual to report, and then eventually I just had to mail in a survey of my current physical condition periodically.

In 1977, the best thing to occur in our lives happened—our first son, Brad, was born. Of all the days in the year, he was born on my mother-in-law's birthday, March 24. What a wonderful gift from God and a wonderful birthday present too! Due to my past surgery, we were advised the probability to have children was unlikely. Nevertheless, God had answered our prayers, and the unimaginable finally happened. Therefore, it began, the family life with each other, playing, working, and praying together. God was giving us a new start and blessing our whole family with this new joy.

Life for our family was hard, just like with most young families. I worked two or more jobs at a time and went to college while Charlene worked for NCH, a large chemical company in Irving, Texas. I was very fortunate to work for Dad Grant as an accounts payable clerk during the day at his grocery firm, Big Value Supermarkets, Inc. On the weekends and on some evenings after school, I prepared tax returns for H R Block during the tax seasons. It seemed as though this was all we ever did on a daily basis just to make ends meet. However, we did manage to take a few vacations when our schedules allowed for them. Over the years, we have wandered across the continental United States from one end to the other. We have visited the most beautiful, curious, and wonderful places this country has to offer.

Our favorite vacation spot is South Dakota, specifically the Mount Rushmore area. However, Texas is our home, and it too has so much to discover and enjoy. With its rich heritage, it will take us an eternity to see it all! We also have very deep roots in this great land. My great-great-grandfather is John Jeremiah "Coho" Smith, who was one of the first Texas Rangers and the first teacher of Parker County. He wrote many journals during his lifetime about his travels and many military engagements. A relative preserved these treasures in a book titled *Coho Graphics*. It tells a lot about this great state and his adventures while riding with the Mexican army. He traveled throughout the land to help make Texas a great republic.

The years continued to fly by, and as God provided, we managed to make most ends meet. Just like most Americans, the dream to own a small home in a friendly neighborhood and to raise a wonderful family was all we needed to make life complete. We have been blessed and could not have asked for anything more.

Just as Sarah and Moses prayed for a son, we too prayed that someday we could give Brad a brother or sister. Time passed, and we were not able to have additional children due to a medical condition as the result of my extensive surgery. As an alternative, we decided to adopt. Charlene and I both agreed this would be the right thing to do—our way of giving back something special to a child in great need. On several occasions, we attempted to adopt a child but to no avail. We either had too many bills or did not have enough income, or too much income, or we heard every excuse imaginable. We eventually gave up and continued to pray for God's mercy. It is so sad that those who want children cannot have them, and sadly, there are those who do not deserve them but have many.

Charlene's sister and husband were having all kinds of marital issues, and they were having difficulty raising their two kids. We would have adopted the children involved, but it probably would have caused more unfavorable issues at the time. It was not the right thing for the kids. So instead, we usually picked them up on the weekends to let them enjoy being kids and to play with their cousin Brad. This not only helped Charlene's sister, but it also gave us the joy of having the kids. Brad was able to feel like he had siblings to play with and grow up with. We would not have had it any other way. If we could not adopt, then it was just as awesome having the relatives around!

It really did not seem fair that we could not have additional kids of our own, but God had a simple solution to our prayers, and He knew what was best for us at the time. Then when Brad was a little over twelve, we got the surprise of our lives! In February 1989, near Valentine's Day, Charlene gave me a note that read ....

"Roses are red, violets are blue. Get ready, Daddy, for Baby Grant number 2."

Charlene was finally pregnant! It was a miracle so unbelievable, but it was true! However, our moment of joy was cut short as Charlene miscarried toward the end of March. It was a huge disappointment, and we were deeply saddened. Toward late September 1989, we were pregnant again. Wow! Even more awesome, she was carrying twins! Early within the pregnancy, once again, she sadly miscarried one of them. Life is just not fair! We were so very distraught. Thereafter, we were very cautious about everything to make certain she would carry the remaining twin to birth. This was so exciting because my brother Sid and his wife, Colleen, were expecting their first child as well! The two cousins would be about six months apart in age and sure to be good friends.

Austin was born to Sid and Colleen in December 1989, and then our second son, Justin Russell, was born on May 31, 1990. Grandma Grant was having a very difficult but humorous time trying to keep the boy's names straight. God blessed her and Dad Grant with two grandsons so suddenly.

Justin Russell came to us miraculously as a prayer answered by God. He looked so much like my deceased brother, Noel. He had the same round face, and he smiled just like him. I have always wondered if Justin was God's way of letting me see Noel one more time. I really believed this in my heart and was to some degree spooked about this special blessing.

Austin and Justin were the perfect two cousins who brought joy and unity to our family. It was so wonderful to have both the boys around to keep us all in laughter as they confused the grandparents as to who was who. It was even more joyful seeing Sid and Colleen being parents for the first time!

After celebrating his thirteenth birthday, Brad was on cloud nine as he finally had a baby brother to hold and to call his own. Justin was a great belated birthday gift for him. Brad did not mind having to wait until May, as he finally got his wish of having a sibling. They bonded well, and Brad could not wait to get up each morning to talk to and play with him. Justin always felt at ease while big brother, Brad, held him in his arms.

Justin was around four weeks old when one difficult night Charlene stayed up rocking him. She thought perhaps he had colic and decided to call the doctor's office early the next morning. Before she was able to call the doctor's office, Justin stopped breathing and fell back into her arms as his little eyes rolled back into his head. He took a deep breath, and she immediately went into panic. She started screaming, "No! No! No!" She laid Justin in his baby bed and starting screaming for Brad to get up and started to call 911. Brad said they could take Justin to the hospital quicker than the ambulance would arrive. Charlene kept running from room to room when Brad mentioned Justin was moaning in his bed. Then they heard him start crying and knew that was a good sign, so they just let him cry. Charlene called the pediatrician and explained what had just occurred. They both hurriedly dressed and rushed Justin to the doctor's office.

The pediatrician met them at the door and took Justin back for an immediate exam. Charlene then called me at work. While crying, she managed to tell me Justin was being admitted to a local hospital in Arlington. Sobbingly she told me he had stopped breathing due to an undetected cause and needed immediate emergency attention.

While at the Arlington hospital, Justin had another episode and stopped breathing again. It was then the emergency staff decided to transfer him to the Fort Worth Cooks Children's Hospital for diagnosis and treatment. I arrived at the emergency room just in time to see Charlene and Justin entering the transfer ambulance. Brad and I took my car and followed the ambulance. I remember thinking the ambulance was going too slow as they drove top speed toward Fort Worth. It was like a slow-motion movie where the actors and events were just barely moving. The only thing flowing at top speed were my tears as I prayed to God that Justin would be okay. I could not help but cry my heart out to God. *Why, Lord, why? Why is this happening? He is just a baby. Please, God, do not take him away from us!*

The turn of events from that day went from meek to a grave situation. We met with so many doctors, surgeons, chaplains, nurses, and specialists that I could not keep track as to who was who. Charlene, Brad, and I prayed for Justin's quick recovery. Then finally, after several hours of nervously waiting, the sad news.

Justin had been born with a major heart condition known as congenital heart disease (CHD). Somewhere in our genetics, Justin had most likely inherited a family trait that was now possibly killing him. We were hurting all over and were very confused as to what was going to happen next. (Congenital Heart Disease is a term that describes a group of heart abnormalities that occur in a fetus before birth. These defects occur while the fetus is still developing and may or may not produce symptoms at birth.)

A wonderful and experienced female heart surgeon from Dallas helped determine the course of treatment. The results of the many tests revealed the two major veins leading from Justin's heart had developed incorrectly, and he had a hole in the wall separating two of his chambers. Surgery could correct the issue, and he might need several follow-up surgeries later as he continued to grow.

It all seemed so simple yet dangerous. Justin was still too weak to have surgery and needed to be at least another week or two older, to get stronger in order to endure the surgery. The wait was so stressful, and everyone in the family was terrified something else would happen before the operation was completed. It was somewhat comforting for us to spend all of our time at the hospital in Justin's room.

The nurses and doctors at Cooks were the greatest and kindest people on earth. They treated us very well and took great care of Justin. Brad was at ease because he could stay with Justin during the day, and he spent the nights at his grandparents'. He did find it unsettling because he could not hold Justin very well with all of the tubes and medical gear attached. We were all so glad Brad was out of school for the summer, so he could spend as much time as possible with his baby brother.

To our comfort, the hospital priest stopped by one day and baptized Justin. He came frequently to pray with us as well. We would go with him to the chapel to pray, and he was so good to Brad. I just knew by going into the chapel something good would come out of all of this. Praying seemed to assure me that God, as always, was in charge and there was to be some hope of Justin getting well.

Since my long ordeal in the hospital several years before, visiting hospitals was not my forte. Living in one again made me feel sick all over, just as it did back then. However, I wanted to be near Justin and needed to support Charlene the best I could. She was taking this situation very hard. One day after sitting for hours, I needed to do something to make the matter a little better to handle. I decided to go to the gift shop to find some kind of toy for Justin.

I found the little gift shop downstairs in the hospital main lobby and started to browse around. Relentlessly scouring over the shop, I did not find anything that struck me as the perfect gift for our baby boy. After a few minutes of feeling lost and frustrated, I started to leave the shop when a sweet elderly woman approached me. She was the perfect volunteer and one you would normally expect to see in a hospital gift shop. She asked if there was something she could help me find. I told her about our little Justin's situation and said I just needed something to help brighten his day as well as ours.

I mentioned to her that nothing available seemed to meet my expectations, because I had scoured the place several times. Somehow, within seconds, she showed me the perfect item. It was a stuffed, bright green and yellow worm with a pull string. Like a kid, I pulled the string, and the music of "Zippity Do Dah" played. It was the perfect toy for Justin. There was plenty of sunshine coming his way, and at that moment, we really did not know how much would be coming. I thanked her for helping me, and she gave me her best wishes. She was going to pray for Justin too.

I felt so much better knowing Justin would enjoy having a stuffed animal to lay beside him during his hospital stay. Charlene and Brad enjoyed pulling the string to play the song for him. Brad enjoyed playing with Justin and tickling his nose with the fuzzy green worm. Justin would just smile and grin each time Brad tickled. It was as if he knew Brad was his older brother as they bonded so well together.

Finally, the day came for the surgery. We were all anxious, and the stress mounted. The operating room nurse came to take Justin away, and something inside me said it would be our last time to tell him we loved him. It was very hard to give him up, but we knew the anticipated surgery was for all the right reasons. Did we make the right decision? Did we do enough to make sure our youngest son would be normal again? The fear was so strong, and the hurting inside each of our hearts was unbearable.

The surgery was to take a few hours, but it seemed like it was taking an eternity. Finally, after four hours, the nurse came to tell us Justin was fine and the surgery was going well. Just a few more hours and the ordeal would be over and then the road to recovery. We were all so ready to go back home with the kids and to move on with our lives.

After several more hours, we were concerned and started to panic. We were beginning to feel that something was wrong, and we needed some kind of assurance everything was going okay. Our adrenaline was soaring. *What is going on?* We needed to see Justin and wanted to speak with the surgeon immediately. Finally, the surgeon came back to report the heart surgery was over. However, baby Justin was having a problem with his little lungs. The surgical team had tried several times during the operation to keep them artificially inflated. Hopelessly, his lungs were beat to a pulp due to the amount of blood they were getting from the oversized artery.

Then the inevitable happened.

The heart surgeon reentered the family waiting room with

obvious tears in her eyes. The operating team could do no more for Justin. She said in a moment he would be prepared for us to go back and see him. Justin had given all he had to fight for his little life, but he could not hold on any longer. Our son, Justin, died at the precious young age of twenty-seven days. How could this be happening? The whole family was simply devastated. The walk back to the room where Justin lay was the longest and hardest walk in my whole life. I tried to keep my composure, but the tears and the agonizing hurt kept coming with every solemn step of the way. Charlene and Brad were crying, and together we all walked the "death trail" to a back room where our newest family member lay, finally without pain. We all lost our hearts and souls that day. I could only repeat over and over, *"My God, my God, why? Precious Jesus, where are you?"* Going home to plan a funeral was not to have been in our itinerary. It was so painful to go home without Justin in our arms that day.

What went wrong? Nothing, any person could repair. God had sent Justin to us temporarily to give us joy, but He needed Justin even more. I still believe to this day Justin was God's way of letting Noel come back into my life to see me one more time. I will always remember the look on Justin's face as I played the little worm song for him. "Zippity do dah, zippity day, plenty of sunshine coming my way." Forever more, Justin has plenty of sunshine to warm his little heart. Even though Charlene, Brad, and I do not have him with us, we too now have plenty of sunshine coming our way. Someday we will be with him again. Someday, our little drop of sunshine, Justin, will be in our arms forever more.

It is as though God was testing our faith just as he had tested Job. I am not certain if we passed or failed; either way, we will always love our God even though we have been hurt to no end with our loss of Justin. Losing a child is one of the most difficult experiences any parent can endure. There were many moments when both Charlene and I were mad at God for taking Justin away from us.

Especially since we had prayed so hard for another child in our lives. We had questioned the authenticity of our faith. We asked ourselves whether perhaps we had deserved this kind of punishment. What was God's purpose in taking Justin from us? Where did we go wrong?

Regardless of the circumstances, Charlene, Brad, and I still have each other, and together we shared that special time with Justin. Very few people ever endure this kind of powerful bonding and the kind of love we have for one another. This challenging experience will never tear our special bonding apart. Our love for each other and those around us continues to grow. We cannot hold anger or hate toward our God because He shares our pain and suffering, and He will continue to bless us regardless. Our God is an awesome God, and He will always be there for us all, no matter what our circumstances.

Before we left the hospital, I wanted to stop by and tell the nice woman in the gift store Justin really enjoyed his little stuffed worm, and to tell her he had passed away. I entered into the gift shop with sadness on my heart and did not see her. I asked the attendants in the shop behind the counter if they knew my friend, but neither one knew of her.

I described her, and they assured me no one fitting my description worked at the shop. They insisted they were the only two volunteers who ran the shop. They also mentioned that the little stuffed worm was not one of their products. Astonished, I left the shop knowing two things. One, the two women must have thought I was crazy. Two, the woman who sold me the little stuffed worm must have been an angel sent by God to warm my heart and to give Justin some peace as well. God had given us all a special miracle meant to remind us of His never-ending love during this very hard moment in our lives.

God works in strange ways to help us through our troubles and sorrows. He is a comforting Father who knows when we need his love and heartfelt companionship. He is there every day in order to help us through the darkest of our days. Through the Holy Spirit, we are given a constant companion who works as our adversary to help us in our time of sorrow, our moments of despair, and when we simply need a direct connection with the Father. One may ask what has the child or parent done in their life that may have caused their child to be born with a defect? Jesus tells us in John 9:3 (KJV)," Neither ... has sinned but this has happened so that the work of God might be displayed in his life."

It is worthy to note God gives us a precious and beautiful gift of life for us to hold in our hands. He allows us to cherish this treasure, to love it, to show it to others, to gloat over it, and then sometimes the unthinkable happens. God reaches down, gently grasps this bundle of joy and beauty, and gently, tearfully takes it away. What was delightfully precious in our hands turns to ashes. Nevertheless, only for a season. For God, as mentioned in Isaiah 61:2–3 (KJV), will "comfort all who mourn, and (will) provide for those who grieve in Zion—to give unto them beauty instead of ashes, the oil of joy instead of mourning, the garment of praise for the spirit of heaviness" when we see Him in glory. In other words, there He will, for eternity, exchange the ashes of life—sadness, mourning, grief, and bitterness for beauty. His beauty and will then hand us the child—our little bundle of joy to hold, cherish, and love for all eternity. Our God is awesome!

> The Lord is nigh unto them that are of a broken heart; and saveth such as be of a contrite spirit.
> —Psalm 34:18 (KJV)

Life Continues and Then There Are Three
Ω

Over the next several years, we watched our family grow in love for one another, and Brad certainly grew to be our pride and joy. God was slowly healing our pains and sorrows. Charlene found a ceramic shop nearby our home and went to work there part-time. She was hoping the craft would help her grieving and ease her anger with God. Brad continued his schooling and challenged himself by bull riding and playing football. I managed to get my MBA after several years of attending college part-time. Finally, we seemed to be completing some our goals in life.

In 1995, Charlene and I were able to collaborate with a close friend and purchased one of Dad Grant's old store locations from years prior. We were proud owners of a grocery store business. However, it proved to be a very physically hard challenge. The rewards of entrepreneurship were positive in many ways, but the long hours were getting the best of the both of us. The frequent sixteen- to eighteen-hour days were taking a toll on my bad leg, causing enormous swelling and pain. With a business note payment hanging over our heads, we had to keep going.

We quickly learned how important it is to communicate with the vendors on a first-name basis, as it was good for business. Some became very close friends. One of these special friends came in one day with such an excitement and glow about her that I had to ask why so much joy. She mentioned a mediator had found her entire biological family of brothers and sisters, mom and dad. She could hardly contain herself. I too was so excited for her and just knew their new relationship would last forever. I asked her for the name of the mediator who helped her, and she gave me a business card that I eagerly placed in my wallet.

The grocery store kept us very occupied, and I simply forgot about the business card. We spent a lot of time working at the store, and there was no personal time for us. Keeping the place running smoothly, controlling the inventory and cash losses, handling the various day-to-day operations, and filling in for absent employees was a major challenge and a royal education.

Charlene was doing her best to help at the store but also knew my sudden desire to find my family as well. Occasionally she was able to go to a local library to do family research and genealogy with her mom. They were good at finding the necessary information and validating the data for accuracy. We have been very blessed to find pictures and stories concerning so many of our ancestors. Especially on Dad Lauderdale's family who had migrated from Scotland. It is so cool to be a part of the Maitland/Lauderdale heritage and have a family castle located in Lauder, Scotland, in the Borders region. Charlene's dad is a direct descendant of the Maitland and Lauderdale ancestry that has occupied the Thirlestane castle for over eight hundred years!

By this time in my life, I started to take more of an interest in finding my own biological family. I guess the excitement Charlene and her mother had toward finding their ancestry must have sparked a flame in my heart as well. I found myself pondering over the paper in my wallet that Mom Grant had given me years before. The more Charlene found on her family, the stronger my desire became. I asked her to see what, if anything, she could find on my family during her road trips and research.

During one of their many outings, Charlene and her mom went to the Fort Worth library to do a little family research. While rumbling through old genealogy records, Charlene overheard a conversation between another researcher and the librarian. She overheard the librarian mentioning a mediator's business card lying on the counter. It was available to the public, and perhaps this mediator might be of additional help to gain information from my adoption records. (A mediator is a professional that assists individuals—perhaps adoptees—to gain access, or at least partial access, to court records by working as a liaison with the judicial system.) Charlene apologized for listening to the conversation but wanted to see if she too could get the business card. The librarian was thrilled to give her one of the cards and spoke highly of the past services she had rendered.

Charlene and I tried several times to obtain my adoption records but never were able to get them. My adoption took place in Tarrant County, officially considered a closed-record county that does not allow records to be released to adoptees. A mediator can sometimes get certain information such as sibling names extracted from the records for medical purposes. On occasion, a few judges will allow some information released as long as the parents' privacy is not compromised. Dealing with the closed-county rules on records angered me to no end. Society's rules on adoption took my childhood years away from my siblings. Nevertheless, we all have to understand and accept the reasoning no matter how painful the outcome.

One day after a long day at work, Charlene presented to me a great gift. She was so excited to share her day with me and was so happy to have received the business card she obtained from the Fort Worth librarian. From time to time throughout our marriage, we had tried to find my siblings and biological family but to no avail. I had given up any hope of finding any of them and just accepted the fact that this was the way it should be.

Charlene handed me the business card. I was startled and could not believe my eyes. "Charlene! You are not going to believe this!" I pulled out of my wallet the same business card I had obtained several months before. We both cried and knew it was a gift from God. He was telling us something, and we needed to listen. It was so supernatural that we both had the same exact card! I promised Charlene to call the mediator. In fact, together we called that very evening.

Mom Grant began to realize that my passion for finding my biological family was growing. With much excitement, she began pushing Dad Grant to obtain my adoption birth certificate, as it had never been received after all of the years I had lived with them. He eventually took the hint and contacted an attorney to help me get it. Of course, we received an adoption certificate with very little true information. At least we knew then my birthplace was in Vallejo, California, and not in Malaga, as I was told for years. Just getting that piece of paper gave me a sense of identity I had never felt before. Just knowing my adoption was legal and truly not a figment of my imagination meant so much. It was the greatest gift Dad Grant had ever given me. I did not realize at the time how important that document would soon become.

Trying to take yet another avenue toward finding my family was always so depressing. So many times, we felt we were getting one step closer and perhaps a name or address of a relative would be just around the corner. However, there were many dead ends with results. The money spent in fees and search agencies and the expense of copies had yielded nothing. Each attempt was just another disappointment, and our hearts were left hurting just a little more. My heart was somewhat blackened by the underlying guilt of even trying to find some resolve to the issue. I am sure every adopted child out there in this cruel world knows exactly the same feeling. The feelings of emptiness, feelings of not belonging, feelings of hurt from not being loved or wanted by a parent. Not to mention the guilty feelings of being a castaway or the root cause of a parental scuffle or ill fate.

Thank God, Charlene is a very strong-willed personality and had enough hope to keep pushing for the both of us. She was determined even more than I was to find my biological family because of her special love for me. I am so thankful God gave me Charlene. I would have given up many times and would never have pursued the challenge without her consistent drive to move forward.

To my surprise, the mediator was very receptive and said it would be nothing to obtain my adoption records, as she worked for the judge who oversaw the adoption court for Tarrant County at the time. I gave her information obtained from the birth certificate Dad Grant provided and the information that Mom Grant had given me years before. I was not certain if any of the information would lead to anyone, but perhaps the mediator could find a fresh, reliable lead.

A few days later, the mediator called the house. I returned the call later that evening, and to my surprise, she had found a sister who was only one year older than I was. What a miracle! She also told me I was not a twin but did have other siblings. Wow! The excitement and adrenalin was rushing to my head. *I have brothers and sisters!* The questions kept coming. *Who are they and where do they live? Can I see them? Do they want to see me? Should I see them? If after our visit, what if they refuse to have anything to do with me? Is it wrong for me to contact them?* There were a hundred more questions and numerous weird thoughts rushing from my brain. *What do we do now?*

The mediator made the arrangements for us to go see my biological sister who lived just about ten miles north of our grocery store. She and her husband lived in north Fort Worth, about thirty miles from our home in Arlington. It was to be an early evening visit a few days after the mediator made the initial contact. Can you imagine the thoughts and excitement Charlene and I had? We both were nervous wrecks, and naturally, we did not know what to expect. The adrenaline was pumping as we walked up to my sister's door for the first time. I was shaking and could have easily run away had it not been for Charlene being with me at the time.

Then, there she was standing in the doorway in a lovely red dress with golden hair. She was so beautiful! I later discovered she and her husband had shopped at our grocery store and we crossed paths many times. Do you remember my mentioning that piece of paper Mom Grant gave me when I was a teenager? Well, it turned out the name on the paper was that of my sister's adopted mother. Sis did grow up in Hurst and attended L D Bell High School. Our schools were archrivals, and we probably saw each other at one of the various football games.

Over time, we were able to get to know each other and become familiar with each other's families. It was so awesome to reminisce about the past and learn how much we all had searched for each other. We shared the numerous stories about the dead-end tips over the years. At the time of our separation, I presume Sis was around two or three years old, and I was around one or two. It had been over forty years since we had seen each other. She remembered more about me than I could ever remember about her. I was just too little at the time.

As time passed, we became very close and shared meals and long conversations with each other's families. One evening, Sis revealed to us she once was in contact with our oldest sister, Michelle.

We learned Michelle at one time provided daycare services. Sis had decided to start providing daycare at her home as well. She needed the money to help balance the family budget. We helped her to set up a large room in her home, and before we knew it, she was licensed and ready to accept several small children. She was in a completely new world, with great enthusiasm and so much vibrant energy. She had registered with the Girl Scouts in order to get her business name out to the local community to build her business.

Then another miracle happened! Sis called me one evening with excitement in her voice. She said a monthly newsletter had arrived in the mail from the Girl Scouts, and to her surprise, the backside listed the names of local daycare providers in the area. We were stunned to find our older sister's name listed as one of the providers. Could it be a listing for another person with the same name? Surely, this was our sister because of the unusual last name. It was a little-known fact that anyone with this same last name had to be a relative. This unusual last name was not a common one, as it was a derivative of her ex's family ancestry from somewhere overseas.

Sis wanted me to call the Girl Scouts and find out more information if possible. Gee. I did not know whom to call, but we did get in touch with the state's agency that was familiar with the newsletter article. The agency referred me to a certain website, and then I started my search by entering the local zip codes. Entering the right zip for the provider's name would then provide the telephone number of the daycare provider.

It took Charlene and me forever one evening to get into the website, but after trying for hours, we made the connection, and we tried every zip code imaginable in the Tarrant County area. Then, after numerous attempts to find the right zip code, the only one left was Euless. We simply could not remember that particular zip code. *"Dear heavenly Father,* I prayed silently, *if you want me to learn more about this daycare provider, and if it is your will that we should make this connection, please reveal to me the final code."* Then the code miraculously came to me—76039 was the final code and the code that opened a door that would change our lives forever! Matthew 6:33 (KJV) says, "But seek ye first the kingdom of God, and his righteousness; and all these things shall be added unto you."

The zip code revealed the full name, address, and telephone

number of a Michelle "K" who lived in Euless, Texas. A registered daycare provider just as Sis had anticipated. She and I were both shocked at the news, and she wondered if I was going to call Michelle. Charlene and I pondered over the information and decided to make the call. It was late in the evening, around nine, and I felt uneasy about calling that late. However, the suspense was killing us both.

Shaking with nervous tension, I dialed the number, and a woman answered. I introduced myself and began to explain how I got her number from the Girl Scouts' daycare provider listing. I began by telling her what my intentions were for calling. It was hard to explain my purpose, and I felt as though I was revealing my guts to a silent ear. The woman began to cry, and I apologized for the interruption, promising not to call again. Before I could hang up, the lady, scolding me, said," Don't hang up!" She began to explain that this particular day, September 23, 1998, was her birthday. In addition, she continued to say while holding back the tears, "This is the best birthday present anyone has ever given to me."

Michelle explained, "I have been looking for you for many years. Over the years, I have spent days at a time searching, but since your name changed so many times, I was unable to find you. I have asked God many times to bring you to me because I simply did not know what else to do." Finally, endless prayers had been answered. God had finally sent her "Robbie" back to her. Over forty years of searching for one another and in just a matter of a few months, two sisters reunited with their brother!

Michelle insisted Charlene and I should come over that night even though it was almost ten. We were very nervous and had reservations about going so late, as we did not know what to expect. We agreed between us, if either of us felt uneasy or the ordeal was a hoax, then we would leave. The plan was to stay together and close to the front door.

The expected address revealed a small home in an older area of

Euless. The home was cute, and the front porch light was on. We walked together toward the door and rang the bell. A short woman answered the door, along with several young kids. Charlene told me her first visual appearance of Michelle was like looking into a mirror image of our younger sister. That miraculous night was so exciting, and we all talked a mile a minute trying to get the most out of it.

Michelle began to tell us she too had a surprise for us. She had called our brother, TJ, and he was coming over immediately. We could not believe it. I had finally come a full circle and now had more family to start knowing and loving.

Charlene could not believe how much TJ and I had in common. She quickly noticed our noticeable mannerisms, our similar looks, and oddly enough, we both have a bum left leg. Awesome! Both siblings talked a mile a minute and were very accommodating. We learned the same family had adopted TJ and Michelle. TJ had suffered from polio, as the adoptive parents would not let them take the vaccine when it was available. He endured severe muscle loss to his left leg, causing a disability and symptoms of post-polio syndrome. His left leg is pencil thin, and he walks with a noticeable limp, as this leg is shorter than the right one.

TJ was very talkative, and we really did not have a lot to say to each other than the usual small talk. We were just trying to adapt to each other. Naturally, we all had a million questions, but we tried to reserve them for a later time, as it was getting very late. We all felt that sense of fear of telling too much about ourselves on our first visit. The instant family was a little overwhelming to take in all at one time. We did exchange phone numbers and agreed to call each other soon.

We hated to leave that night, as it felt like a dream. However, after meeting a newfound sister and brother and several nieces and nephews, it was just too much to take in for one night. What about the next day? Where would this newfound love lead us? Would we find our mom and dad as well? Will there be other relatives soon revealed?

God had touched all of us and blessed us with this great reunion. What more could we ask? "He is our shepherd, and we shall not want."

It had been a very long day, as neither Charlene nor I had slept much due to the excitement. Naturally our minds were racing with all of the various questions and what-ifs. Stunned, we had to pinch ourselves once again to make sure we were not dreaming. It is amazing how a simple newsletter turned out to be the key to opening this great door.

The days following led to an amazing family reconnection, and the bonding began to flourish. So many questions and thoughts would come up, and we did our best to make the best of it all. Michelle and TJ spoke of old memories that soon started to surface from the past as we continued to visit with each other. We were astonished as to all of the close encounters that came our way. Many times, we had crossed paths at schools, churches, and events. We even lived within a few miles of each other! At any point in time, we could have spoken to each other and would have never known our biological relationship.

One main question was still on all of our minds: where were our parents? We would ask ourselves if they could possibly be alive, and if so, would they know us? Our next mission as newly founded siblings was to find our parents and quickly. We were puzzled as to where to start our search.

Michelle, who is the oldest sibling, was born in Sydney, New York. She traveled with our mom and dad while growing up. She remembered Leroy, our dad, was originally from Upstate New York, as was his immediate family. Charlene had remembered that during a previous trip to California as well. Armed with this information, we decided our next mission would be to try to locate Dad somewhere in New York.

We sent letters to the state of New York's vital statistics department inquiring about Leroy. Since all of the siblings' last names changed due to their adoptions and were not the same as Dad's last name, the agency refused to send us any information. We did not know if he was alive or dead. Michelle also recalled Dad and his family were from an area south of Rochester. Several attempts to locate him using other resources ended up in dead ends. Now it appeared as though my three siblings and I were going to be the limit to our newfound family. Charlene and I were very content with just having them in our lives, and what a remarkable blessing!

However, the Lord had other plans in the making. I truly believe He wanted to give us the path to finding Dad, but our goals were probably not at the top of his list. This reminds me of Deuteronomy 30:3–5 (KJV) that says He will, "have compassion upon thee, and will return and gather thee from all the nations ... the Lord thy God will bring thee into the land which thy fathers possessed, and thou shalt possess it; and he will do thee good, and multiply thee above thy fathers."

Shockingly, my beloved Mom Grant passed away in late November 1995. Sid and I lost an important part of our lives. Her passing made a deep wound in our hearts. Slowly our precious past seemed to be slipping away with the passing of this loving family member. It took me a long time to adjust to this additional loss. Mysteriously though, soon after Mom Grant's passing, another series of unusual happenings began to take place. Since that day of our flower garden episode, she always knew what lingered deep within my heart. Special events started to occur that miraculously opened up doors toward finding more biological family ties. It seemed as though she was angelically directing unusual things to happen. Charlene and I began on a very unusual path toward finding more family.

> Behold, how good and how pleasant it is for brethren to dwell together in unity.
> —Psalm 133:1 (KJV)

A Mother Is Found

Ω

Michelle told us our mother's family was originally from Bridgeport, Texas, and she knew her maiden name. She suggested we go to Bridgeport to see if any of the family still lived there. Perhaps we could locate someone who knew one of the family members and we might get a lead on our mom.

Ready for a road trip, Charlene, her parents, our niece, and I headed out on the road but this time toward Bridgeport to see if we could discover relatives or information about them. Fortunately for us, Bridgeport is a small community located south of a slightly larger city known as Decatur. Bridgeport was a striving coal mining town years ago, and the mining company was the major employer. The economy of the town shut down when the mining company closed. A longstanding labor dispute was to blame. In addition, the city used to be one of the main stops for the Butterfield Stagecoach. Since Bridgeport was just a few miles west of Fort Worth, it was a welcomed resting spot for weary travelers going to Dallas. Eventually the trains replaced the stagecoach, and the town suffered from the lack of continual migration into area.

When we arrived in town, the first place visited was a local convenience store on the main highway. I mentioned to the cashier what we were doing in Bridgeport and asked if she knew any of the family members. She confirmed a Reverend Bill was a close friend and suggested we check the local phone book for other possible relatives. Reverend Bill was the chaplain for the Runaway Bay Fire Department. Runaway Bay is a small community on Lake Bridgeport.

Unbelievably there were boatloads of the family listed in Bridgeport! Where do we start? Whom should we go see first, and what do we say to a stranger? The best place to get started was the first name listed in the telephone book under our mother's maiden name. First up, "Adam." (For privacy purposes and due to his health condition, I have changed his first name.) So it was agreed upon, and we set out to find Adam. We all prayed this person would know someone related to our mom. Was it possible? I was beginning to believe that miracles could happen to us at just about any time. After all, we had testimony to so many during our lives so far.

We were having problems trying to find the right street and had made several wrong turns. GPS was not affordable at the time, so we had to rely on the old-fashioned maps. We managed to find a young man working on a car down one of the many side streets. He was kind enough to stop and chat with us for a moment. He gave us the right directions and told us he was Reverend Bill's son. He also told us that Adam was his uncle. We were a little unsure if we were actually looking for the right family, but at least this was a great lead.

Soon after our brief visit, we found Adam's home. Charlene and I nervously walked up to his door and knocked. A sweet woman arrived at the door, and we asked to speak with Adam. Naturally, the woman was unsure of us and indicated that he had been ill and might not want to talk to us. I explained with great uncertainty that we might be related. To our surprise, Adam came to the door and invited us all to come inside to his dining room. He offered us cool drinks and seemed very excited to see us.

We began to explain why we were intruding on this peaceful evening and how we felt he might be able to assist us. Before I went into my dialogue, he began by acknowledging he knew who I was, and furthermore he knew Darlene (Michelle's birth name). He asked about Darwin (TJ's birth name) and said that he knew about the adoptions and the reason behind the splitting up of the family. This really caught me off guard, and I was speechless to learn he knew who I was. He must have known me when I was very young. Nevertheless, what a relief to have found a blood relative that knew our family history!

After a few minutes of conversation, Reverend Bill showed up. It is then we learned the reverend was indeed one of our uncles. He appeared to be very soft-spoken, reserved, and cautious to speak. He did confirm his position as the chaplain for the Runaway Bay Fire Department and went into detail about his duties within the department. What a great guy!

The visit had Charlene and I so excited we had simply forgotten about her parents sitting in the van. We thanked all of the newly found relatives for letting us visit and for being so receptive. It was great to have actually visited with biological relatives. What a day!

Adam told us a world of information that would eventually lead us to my biological mom. The address we were given was near the ceramic shop where Charlene had worked in the past. I cannot believe we passed Mom's house all of those years! In a way, this was exciting news, but then again, I was saddened, as I could have known her many years ago.

Uncle Adam had told us Mom might not answer her front door bell and to simply leave a note on the back door. Just as Adam said, she would not answer her door, and it was very understandable. She did not know Charlene and me, and I would not answer the door either. We left a note with our contact numbers just in case she wanted to call. Strangely, I was content knowing where Mom lived, but I was questioning whether or not she wanted anything to do with my siblings or me.

A few weeks later, God answered a lifelong prayer. Mom called Charlene and talked to her for almost five hours! They talked about everything from the past to the present. As I walked in from work that day, I noticed Charlene was talking on the phone, and quietly I asked who it might be. Charlene whispered, "Your mom wants to talk to you." I thought, *Who?* Then she quickly handed me the phone, and fear went throughout my body like a lightning bolt. What do you say to someone whom you really do not know but you have been seeking for over forty years? You just stutter in disbelief and ramble. "Ugh, Mom?"

I could tell the uneasiness in her voice as we both said hello. The conversation went well, and after an hour, I could tell the nervous tension was gone and the inquisitive side of our conversation began. The small talk was flowing because neither one of us knew exactly what to say. We both wanted to talk again and knew that this reunion needed to move slowly and cautiously. After we hung up, I did not know how I felt. I was more stunned than anything and figured it would be a long time before our next conversation. It was important to me not to move too quickly with questions about the past, as I did not want to invade her privacy or appear to be too eager to get answers fast. It was best to move slowly and to get to know each other a little better before asking any prying or hard questions. In due time, the answers would come, and the bonding process would begin.

I asked myself, *Did this just happen?* Charlene was far more excited than I was. She could not wait to tell everyone about our evening. How awesome it was finally to talk to my real mom. After several days, we were still talking about the six hours of conversation. Where would this event lead us? When would the next conversation take place? Would a face-to-face meeting come?

My forty-fifth birthday was coming up, and I knew something big was going to happen as Charlene was on pins and needles several days before. It was going to be a special day as always. We looked forward to having a cookout, ice cream, and cake. The little kid in me really comes out on my birthday! I never really wanted anything, but whatever Charlene and Brad planned was always special, and I did not have to worry about not having a good time.

The big day came, and Charlene's dad and mom came over to help us celebrate. I was looking forward to cooking hamburgers and having fun. I could tell Charlene was feeling a little nervous for some reason. I did not think she was in pain or was sick. The cookout was going well, and her dad was hanging outside with me. I always prepare too much food, but if anything was left over, it was consumed the next day by taking it to school or work for lunches.

Finally, I completed the cooking, and Charlene came to the back door to tell me that someone wanted to see me. I walked into the house to deliver the great-smelling burgers and dogs. As I entered, I noticed two unfamiliar people in our family room. Not knowing who they were, I set down the pan of food to go and introduce myself. All along, I was thinking they were salespersons or folks visiting from the neighborhood. Charlene then introduced the two strangers, and to my surprise, my mom and half sister were standing before me. Praise God! How in the world did Charlene ever get this accomplished? She said that it took a lot of convincing and pleading, but Mom finally agreed to come.

At first, Mom was a little hesitant to give me a hug and likewise. I knew in order to bond after some forty odd years, what could a hug hurt? I did not feel any sparks flying, and even though the moment of closeness was short, that certain feeling only a Mom and a child can feel became a sudden reality. (I remembered then what Mom Grant had mentioned years ago about a child needing his or her family.) I knew in time the bonding would grow and any fear or uneasiness first encountered would soon fade. This moment reminded me of the many pictures of Christ portrayed as a baby, being held by His mom, the blessed Virgin Mary, thus reflecting a special bond every human needs to experience. So many children miss this special moment, a point in time yielding the greatest feeling of oneness. A moment of comfort and peace, a glimpse of time without fear and worries. A special bonding between a mother and her child.

Mom and my half sister, Cheryl, became at ease during the evening as we all ate our meal and talked about the many events in our lives. Mom told us that it was several years after the placement of all of the initial children that she met an established restaurant owner, Charles. They decided to get married, and together they started a wonderful family with three additional kids to raise, and this time for keeps. Cheryl told us about her two brothers. Charlene and I had the opportunity to meet them later. We did not know how everyone would accept us, but over time we began to love one another very much.

Only God knows how many times I must have passed Mom's house in Fort Worth through the years growing up. As mentioned earlier, Charlene had passed her house many times going to work in Fort Worth. You may have heard the old adage, "Once you have been adopted, your biological family is not far away." Sure enough, mine was in my backyard for many years. Finally, with divine intervention, we crossed paths.

Having Charlene's parents with us made the evening feel special. Mom felt comfortable talking to them, as they were around the same ages and each had endured the hard but good ole days. Time flew by, and it was nearly one o'clock in the morning. Mom did not want to leave, as she was so excited about the evening and finally getting to meet Charlene and me. She talked about her deceased husband and my other half siblings. I just knew that Cheryl was a special person to have brought Mom to the party. She was so understanding and yet inquisitive as well. What a birthday gift!

I knew deep inside my heart that Mom Grant would be beaming like a possum knowing I had finally connected to my biological mom. I bet she earned her wings that day. Somehow, she knew that this day would come even though as a young teen it really had not mattered to me. Nevertheless, after this gathering, I finally realized what she meant so many years ago, and for that, the moment was priceless.

It was a special birthday gift from God.

> Strength and honour are her clothing; and she shall rejoice in time to come. She openeth her mouth with wisdom; and in her tongue is the law of kindness. She looketh well to the ways of her household, and eateth not the bread of idleness. Her children arise up, and call her blessed.
> —Proverbs 31:25–28 (KJV)

Extended Family

Ω

The bonding of a once displaced family continues to this very day, and new memories begin as each member indulges to learn about the other. Many questions from the past are answered, and new ones arise. At this point, the missing link to this miraculous comeback is Dad. Where is he? Can he be found?

After all of these years, Mom had only one picture of Dad remaining in her possession. It was a severely wadded picture, as she still had it in an old purse in the back of her closet. The black-and-white photo was in bad condition, and getting it reconstructed would be close to impossible. Charlene and I took it to a local photography shop with prayers they could refurbish the photo to a somewhat fair condition. After a few weeks, the photo was completed, and we were amazed! Finally, we had a clear picture of my dad after decades. I did not take after him; however, TJ was a twin image. The reconstructed photo revealed a short but handsome young man wearing a light-colored suit and dark tie. Mom commented that he was so proud of his full head of dark hair and his stylish pompadour haircut that was classic of the times. The picture shows him standing in front of a dated home, possibly owned by a relative.

Just a couple of months after finding Mom, we all attempted to determine whether Dad was deceased. Michelle and I sent letters requesting both a death certificate and a birth certificate. The state of New York politely refused to answer our requests since we did not have the same last name. This was so frustrating!

We also sent letters to libraries requesting information but to no avail. Michelle then came up with the brilliant idea to call a library in a small town in Upstate New York. Once again, God performed another miracle that would astound us all!

Michelle was able to speak with a librarian somewhere in the area of Dansville. The librarian was interested in knowing why the call. After Michelle explained the situation and reiterated the names and other details, the librarian advised Michelle to call a county clerk. The librarian gave her another number to call, thus leaving Michelle in a position of curiosity and frustration once again.

Determined to find Dad, Michelle called the county number as given and spoke with a certain Shirley. By the grace of God, Shirley not only had known our dad, but she also attended church with his sons. At this point, there was a little ray of hope that we might be just a little closer to seeing our dad for the first time in years. Shirley was accommodating and had our half brother call Michelle. Talking about a miracle, we found the other side of our missing family! After speaking with our half brother, he revealed that Dad had passed away a few years earlier. We were all devastated to learn that we would never get to see him. It was then our journey of hope had seemingly come to a bitter end.

It was not long before Michelle, TJ, and I booked a flight to New York to visit our dad's other family. We flew from DFW to Buffalo. Unexpectedly, we were all bumped due to the number of passengers that were overbooked for the upcoming flight. Our tickets were standby, and this was going to cause us to wait for another flight. In the meantime, Michelle was busy trying to find another way to get us to Buffalo.

Meanwhile we were PUSH-ing (praying until something happened). While we were waiting for Michelle, I was telling one of the flight attendants why we were flying to New York and how we were fortunate to find our extended family. While being so emotionally moved by our story, the flight attendant felt compelled to try to do something to get us on that plane. She went to the captain to explain our situation. The pilot, a believer himself, asked us to come aboard the plane. They placed us in the near-empty first-class section, and we were off to Buffalo! God was still working his miracles! Our adrenaline was excitingly pumping!

The flight to Buffalo was awesome, and without any further issues, we were able to rent a car to drive to our destination. We were all nervous wrecks by the time we arrived at our motel. We called our oldest half brother, who quickly met us at the motel. We then followed him to his country home where we met more anxiously waiting family members.

The family took us on a small tour of the town of Nina, a quaint, historical Methodist church, and the cemetery across the road where we viewed our dad's final resting place. Barely noticeable was a small identification plate mounted on the ground, reflecting his departure in 1995. (Mom Grant had passed that same year. Somewhat peculiar if you ask me.) It was unsettling that he had been buried before we had a chance to meet him in person—or to have a special bonding conversation.

As I stood there looking at his plot, I felt a little uneasy. It was as if something was tugging at my heart, as if to say, "I am so sorry." I could not cry; nor could I scream out or even feel anger. I was in disbelief as to where I was standing. After all of the years that Charlene and I tried to find him, it was another let down. Was I standing at his grave for real, or was I living a dream? All I could do was say a little prayer for him and tell him how sorry I was for not getting to him sooner. Now the many unanswered questions would continue to spin within each of our heads. In a way, I was glad not to have had that conversation because of my mixed emotions. Then again, I would not have wanted to disappoint Dad in any way. The unanswered questions—would he have been proud of all of us? Alternatively, had we had met prior to his death, would he have turned us away? Did he still love us? Could I have shown him my love? Could my brother and sisters forgive him for everything that happened in the past?

Our visit with the extended family turned out to be remarkable. We were able to meet all of the nieces and nephews and a very special woman, our stepmother. Dad had actually built the house where she was living from the trees that stood around the home. A wonderful single story with a huge basement. It had a spectacular picture window at the front of the house with a beautiful view of the forestry surrounding the area. (I evidently inherited my carpenter skills from Dad, as I too love working with wood.)

The newfound family could not believe how much TJ resembled Dad. They were so shocked by the similarities and felt as though they were seeing Dad's ghost. (TJ got his musical ability from Dad as well.) Our Texas mom had located a 45-rpm record Dad had recorded years ago and gave it to TJ. The record is not the best in the world, but it reveals our dad's voice, something the Texas family was fortunate to hear for the first time.

I have not seen my dad since my early toddler days and have wondered for years if he ever missed my siblings and me. I often wondered if he carried pictures of us. Did he go to bed at night wondering where we were or if we had food to eat or clothes to wear? Numerous questions like these remain on the lips of the once loved ones left behind. Standing near his grave left us with some peace and the solitude that we knew where he is forever.

Nothing hurts more than not knowing your biological parents and siblings while growing up as a child. For many, the deep and empty feeling of not sharing their love and company forever eats at one's soul. Since I have not seen my real dad for over sixty years, missing him still brings tears to my eyes, even today.

On the way back home, my mind was trying to absorb all that had transpired over the last several months. It was as if my life had been set in a fast-forward motion with so much being revealed at a very fast pace. I felt my mind was overloaded and did not know what to expect next. God was answering so many prayers quickly, and He was revealing so much heartfelt information to us all. It was as though God wanted us to get all of the past behind us so that we could move forward with our lives.

Just to think, a few months prior to visiting Dads' grave, I only had one living brother, and now I had numerous sisters and brothers. Keeping up with them all has become a wonderful challenge. Keeping their names and their family member names straight is a big challenge, as my memory is now starting to fail me. However, having this large extended family has been a wonderful blessing, and the joy of experiencing each newfound member is a gift only God can give.

According to the Child Welfare Information Gateway, there were over 135,800 children in the United States given up for adoption in 2008 as the result of the various states' CPS actions or for other reasons, too many to mention. However, our God, who keeps an eye on even the little sparrow that falls to the ground, certainly knows of every child that falls victim of abuse, neglect, anger, and/ or separation from his or her parents or siblings for whatever reason. Psalm 27:10 (KJV) assures, "When my father and my mother forsake me, then the Lord will take me up."

We must pray for the fathers and mothers of this generation, and for others to follow, that many will come to know God the Father and in a more personal way. Parents have such a hard time finding work and keeping finances under control, and they have less time for loving each other. Pray they will learn God's holy Word, thereby giving them strength, hope, and power over the enemy (the one who seeks to destroy us) and letting them stand firmly together, united with Christ, our redeemer!

Sing unto God, sing praises to his name: extol him that rideth upon the heavens by his name JAH, and rejoice before him. A father of the fatherless, and a judge of the widows, is God in his holy habitation.
—Psalm 68:4–5 (KJV)

In Closing—Love Thy God
Ω

My life has come full circle since the days of the seemingly never-ending dream many years ago. I never dreamed our Lord would send so many blessings my way. It is amazing how my life has changed so much in such a remarkably short period—from the time I grew up with two awesome brothers in a small town, to changing into a man during the Viet Nam War, to getting married and having a family of my own. Despite the hardships, God has given me a lot of love and more blessings than any one person fully deserves.

Finding my biological family had been a distant dream and an annual hopeless birthday wish. It is amazing how the numerous clues and hints revealed during my life suddenly merged to make the repeated wishes become a reality. I fully believe God executed these miracles in my life. Each special event has taught me a little more about life and death, love and faith. The valuable knowledge and wisdom we learn during our lives is definitely what God wants us to embrace in order to do his will and to find our way to heaven.

Many in this world today think God is not in touch with them. It is true that even today there are those who believe in many gods, and many claim to be atheist or whatever. However, if one would simply ... be still and know He is God ... then many will see how He too touches each of us in many ways. Just look around. Do you see the love and kindness in our spouses, our children, our siblings, our parents or grandparents, our pastors and teachers? Moreover, through the Holy Spirit, God is working through each one of us. If we offer a simple act of kindness, offer a loving hand, or share a purely compassionate heart, we too are giving a potential blessing from the one true God to another. God grants us the free will to love Him and to love each other. Whether or not we accept this gift depends on our commitment to believing in Him and accepting His grace.

I am reminded of a great silver leaf maple tree growing in our backyard. Years ago, when we first planted this great tree, it was a small, five-foot, scrawny thing. It was all we could afford at the time, as we had just purchased our home and did not have the extra cash to buy such things. I think we spent twenty-five dollars or less and were hoping for the best. Another previously planted tree had died just shortly before this replacement.

A few weeks after we planted this second tree, a big Texas storm cropped up out of nowhere. This is common during the spring and usually comes with high winds, a lot of rain, and sometimes hail stones the size of baseballs. As expected, there was a lot of thunder and lightning, enough to wake the dead! The next morning presented itself to be a gorgeous day. A reminder God is in control of everything, and He is always there to see we make it through the roughest of storms in life.

I was out early the day following the storm to survey for damages, and sure enough, we had a casualty. Lightning had struck our only tree! It was zapped right smack in half and had been burned to a charcoal black from the middle up. God is certainly an excellent sharpshooter! He gave this tree a taste of His power, and I just knew it would probably not survive. The top half of this poor tree lay helplessly bent over and leaning onto the ground. I was so upset over the matter. Charlene and I decided to break off the top half and leave the rest in the ground. If the poor thing lived, then great!

If it was completely dead, then it would be awhile before we could afford to replace it.

Today, I cannot put my arms around the trunk of this great majestic beauty. It is taller than three stories and has lived to be over forty years old! This is very uncommon for a maple tree. I have always pondered over its unusual giant size. It proudly stands as a reminder of our God who is all-powerful and who shows us how his touch can change lives. I love this old tree because God continually uses it to display an important message to our family. He wants us to ... be still and know that He is God ... for He is the only true God. This mighty tree shades our home and yard, reaffirming God's love for us. He takes his mighty hands and covers us with His protection from harm's way.

Every year, this mighty tree sheds its leaves in the autumn to magically fall into a well-earned deep sleep. This dreary, gray-looking giant has intelligently prepared itself for the bitter-cold winters ahead, hoping to survive once again without any harm to its branches. Simply standing and waiting for the spring to come once again and patiently waiting for a new life ahead from its maker.

In the real world, we too should follow the example of the trees. We need to frequently stop and simply take a break. Most of us have such consuming lives running the kids to school, rushing to meetings, playing sports, studying for tests, or preparing for that once-in-a-lifetime opportunity. Nevertheless, do we stop long enough to be aware of our surroundings, to simply listen and reflect on what God wants us to do? How often do we stand still and put our lives on hold to prepare for the future the way God wants us to live? Do we attend church or do we shortly stop in our tracks long enough to thank Him for our many blessings?

Seasonally, the trees know when to come alive each spring as they burst into a bright green growth of new leaves and extended branches. It is as though they logically calculate when to spring into life, thus renewing themselves after the sleepiness of winter. Faithfully, they reach for the sky, as high as they can, in order to worship and to thank God for giving them a renewed life once again. Each new branch yields great strength and bursts with compassion to provide for a playful family of squirrels or for a new bird's nest, a new life.

To truly know our God, we must submit our whole selves to Him, both physically and mentally. We are to love and obey Him. We should stop our busy lives to worship Him daily. To help us stay on the right growth pattern, to yield strong branches for one another, God has given us the Holy Spirit. When we reach out our arms to God and devote our lives to Him, it is then we realize how all-loving and caring He is to us. The Holy Spirit is God's special way of physically touching each of us.

Embrace the Holy Spirit and thank God for giving us this special gift. Pray often to God and ask Him to help you to do His will, to live by His commandments, and to be more like Him. Like the trees, we too should look up each day and reach out for our God, thus giving Him the thanks and the praise He worthily deserves. Study His word by frequently reading the Bible. Find a good Bible-based church and develop a church family. Live the dream and look for the miracles in your life. Stretch out your arms and reach for God! Then love Him with all of your heart and let the comforting finger of God Almighty touch you. Shalom.

> For I am persuaded, that neither death, nor life, nor angels, or principalities, nor powers, nor things present, nor things to come, nor height, nor depth, nor any other creature, shall be able to separate us from the love of God, which is in Christ Jesus our Lord.
> —Romans 8:38–39 (KJV)

Additional Reading

Grandmother Johnson was right on! Heaven is beautiful! We all have sat and pondered about heaven and the questions associated with it. Perhaps we were in conversation while among family or friends when the subject was brought up for discussion. What does the Bible have to say about our God's house?

In biblical terms, heaven is a place of everlasting, blessedness of the righteous, and the abode of parted spirits:

A. Christ called it "His Father's House"—John 14:2

B. Sometimes called "Paradise"—Luke 23:43, 2 Cor. 12:4, and Rev. 2:7

C. Heavenly Jerusalem—Galatians 4:26, Hebrews 12:22, and Rev. 3:12

D. Abraham's Bosom—Luke 16:22

E. The Kingdom of Heaven—Matthew 25:1, James 2:5

F. The Eternal Inheritance—1 Peter 1:4, Hebrews 9:15

G. The Better Country—Hebrews 11:14–16

Here are just a few examples of books written by those who have had a glimpse of heaven and yet returned to earth to give testimony:

A. *My Glimpse of Eternity* by Betty Malz. Betty had been on vacation with her family in Florida when she noticed extreme pain in her side. She first thought it was just because of a pulled muscle; however, the pain continued to get worse. She realized something was seriously wrong. Betty then died but returned to life to share her incredible testimony!

B. *Ninety Minutes in Heaven* by Don Piper. It was 1989. Reverend Piper was on his way home from a minister's conference when a semitruck that had crossed over into his lane crushed his car. While his body lay lifeless inside the mangled car, Piper experienced heaven. Ninety minutes after the wreck, another minister prayed for him. Piper miraculously came back to life, having had a glimpse of heaven! Then his gruesome recovery began.

C. *Heaven Is for Real* and *Heaven Changes Things* by Todd Burpo. Todd's three-year-old son, Colton, had an incredible journey to heaven during an emergency surgery and met with his grandfather and a sister who he had passed away before Colton was born. Colton was not aware of the sister's death prior to going to heaven.

These are a few wonderful scriptural references written to help us overcome our fears:

A. Psalm 23:—The Lord is my Shepherd (KJV)

B. Psalm 23:4, Psalm 91:1–16, and John 16:33 (KJV)

C. Genesis 49:24—The Shepherd—Rock of Israel (KJV)

D. Hebrews 13:20—That Great Shepherd of the Sheep (KJV)

E. Deuteronomy 31:6—"Be strong and of good courage, fear not, nor be afraid of them: for the Lord thy God, he it is that doth go with thee; he will not fail thee, nor forsake thee" (KJV).

F. Proverbs 18:24—"A man that hath friends must shew himself friendly: and there is a friend that sticketh closer than a brother" (KJV).

The Rev. Charles H. Spurgeon wrote his sermon #148 on the "Five Fears" on August 23, 1857 at the music hall in Royal Surrey Gardens addressing the five fears:

1. The fear caused by an awakening conscience
2. The fear of anxiety
3. A fear that works caution
4. The fear of jealousy
5. Fear felt when we have divine manifestations

The adoption of a child or teenager may not always be the right decision for parents-to-be. Many times, the process is cumbersome and expensive. It is not always evident or visible that the prospective son or daughter has physical limitations, emotional scars, or mental issues that may need special consideration or treatment. Some issues do not reveal themselves until days or even years after the adoption takes place. These kinds of issues can subject the prospective parents to additional financial stress or even cause issues with existing family members.

It is always best to secure a full background check on the biological family in order to obtain as much information as possible, to determine any issues or possible abuse that may have been experienced by the adoptee.

It takes a very special family to adopt an unwanted or misplaced child. The need to place these special persons is great. There are many churches and organizations that can assist in answering the sometimes-difficult questions that need to be answered before an adoption takes place. It is important to discuss these with your ministers, friends, and relatives both before and during the adoption process. A well-informed and educated parent-to-be will make a better future for all parties involved.

Remember too, someday after the adoption takes place, the

adoptee will want to know the truth about his or her biological family. Eventually they will have many questions requiring answers in order to have peace of mind. Be honest and supportive. Answer the questions truthfully and the best you can.

Consider fostering a child first. Then weigh the pros and cons, the needs and wants of the child or teen, and make your decision based on prayer. It takes a special person to want to adopt someone else's child. I have always believed that adoption is a selfless act of love. It is a pro-life alternative to abortion. I could have been aborted, and I am so thankful that my mom carried me to birth. She gave me a fighting chance to live a better life. Thank you, Mom!

Printed in the United States
By Bookmasters